BEYOND
Beautiful

To Angela —
I hope you enjoy
the book! Thank you
for your support. It
means a lot.
Peace & Blessings ~
Nancy

Beyond Beautiful Endorsements

This book is all about courage – the courage to survive challenges, explore one's own inner self, significantly change thoughts and behavior, and finally, the courage to be in the world as an empowered woman. Each author shares her deeply personal journey of struggles, awakening moments, and breakthroughs. You will laugh and cry and ultimately find in their words the courage to move forward in your own journey to wholeness.

~ Patricia J. Crane, Ph.D., Author, speaker and trainer
www.drpatriciacrane.com

Beyond Beautiful is a powerful resource for those of us seeking to heal ourselves. The simple yet effective tools mentioned, along with personal stories by contributors Nancy Newman, Lisa Hardwick, Elaine Lemon, Robyn Podboy, and Cindy Ray enrich this uplifting book. My deepest gratitude to all the authors for sharing their knowledge and insights.

~ Susanne Marie Knight, Award-winning author
www.susanneknight.com

The authors of *Beyond Beautiful* offer deep insights into life's experiences, joyful as well as sorrowful; in addition, they will guide you in the art of affirmation regarding the choices you desire to make in your life. If you want to discover how to forgive and accept yourself as the beautiful person you are inside and out, then this book will become a symbol of hope and will provide instructions and examples to guide you through the process of renewal and healing.

~ Tammy G. Lagoski , Publishing Consultant and Published Author

I laughed, I cried, and I realized that I could re-create my life filled with love, laughter, fun and hope. Reading the real life stories of these beautiful women inspires you and allows you to see that you can make changes too! Their experiences will guide you and teach you on how to re-create your life; the life that you've dreamed of living.

~ Terry Reem, Heal Your Life® Teacher and Life Coach

This is a truly informative book sure to inspire many as the authors share their personal journeys towards health and healing, and how they literally "changed their minds." An engaging work from start to finish that guides you in the steps necessary to create the beautiful life you desire!

~ Kimberly S. Pratte, Reiki Master/Teacher and
Co-author of "Restoring Your Beautiful Life"

In *Beyond Beautiful*, the authors present thoughtful discussions and practical guidance that teach us that when we release our painful past histories, we take power over our present. Through this process which is presented in every chapter, we can create an opportunity to become our most glorious, authentic selves. We learn by their examples how to embrace the challenge of forgiveness and reap the benefits of true inner healing. We learn about the impact that our personal beliefs and thoughts have on our destinies, and how they can interfere with our desire to live our dreams to the fullest. Through self examination and discovery, we are given the opportunity to recognize our unique divine essence and to embrace our challenges as gifts that reveal life's many lessons. The autobiographical stories of transformation are encouraging, uplifting, and promising. Through the process of sharing their personal stories, the authors graciously give us a glimpse of their own intimate journeys of healing. Through their experiences we can relate to the universal lessons that are revealed. You will be moved by the loving compassion presented within these pages.

~ C.P. Bottrell, Ph.D. is the author of Living The Mystery: Exploring Universal Wisdom and Our Connection to the Divine. Dr. Bottrell is an associate professor of Psychology, an educational and clinical psychologist, and an ordained Interfaith Minister. She lives and works both in the United Kingdom and the United States.

The principles exemplified in Beyond Beautiful are a message of forgiveness, healing and recognition of your own inner beauty. Through the authors' trials, tribulations and triumphs we gain the strong message that we are ENOUGH as we are. The authors' inspired words touched my heart, reinforcing my courage to walk through the fire and embrace my fears in order to experience someone that has always been and will always be there, my powerful and beautiful true Self. Beyond Beautiful teaches us to embrace life and affirm the greatness within us.

~ Michael Karlfeldt, N.D., Ph.D., owner and founder of Swedish Naturopathic and Karlfeldt Healing Retreats, empowering and changing lives one at a time

It seems to me that everyone is going through major life-altering changes at this time. If you are not now, you soon will be; because that is the time in which we have chosen to live. The question is "what are you going to do with those changes?" In *Beyond Beautiful*, the authors share insights into spiritual awakening and growth; better health; and emotional balance. As we look for ways to mine these growth opportunities, the authors' unique training and experiences provide tools for maximizing your spiritual growth and healing. Whether you feel like you are just awakening to your journey or you feel like you have been at it for decades, you will be blessed by *Beyond Beautiful*. I encourage you to read this book and follow up with the authors to experience all they have to offer.

~ Robert K. Banks, Publisher; TheMemoryShirt.com; Retired Executive Vice President, Albertsons, Inc.

I, myself, am a licensed *Heal Your Life* ® teacher and the stories in this book not only offered me a refresher course in all that I believe and teach, it opened my eyes and taught me some new valuable ways of thinking!

~ Shelly York, Licensed Heal Your Life® Teacher

Beyond Beautiful is an incredible testament to self-healing. Written by women who transformed their difficult life experiences; they share candidly from their hearts to inspire and empower others. A must read for all in transition.

~ Candess M. Campbell, Ph.D
www.candesscampbell.com

❝OUR *habitual behavior*

derives from SOMETHING that

happened to us in the PAST that

led us to BELIEVE certain things

about OURSELVES. Now is a

GREAT time for CLOSURE.

Today is a PERFECT day to

re-write our script

and START OVER. ❞

~Lisa Hardwick

BEYOND

Beautiful

BECKWORTH PUBLICATIONS

3108 E 10th St. ~ Trenton, Mo 64683 ~ 660-204-4088

Ordering information: Quantity Sales. Special discounts are available on quantity purchases by corporations, associations, and others. For details, contact the "Special Sales Department at Beckworth Publications."

Beckworth Publications and the Beckworth Publications logo are trademarks of Beckworth Publications.

Printed in the United States of America.

Library of Congress Cataloging-in-Publication Data.

Hardwick, Lisa
Beyond Beautiful: Five Amazing Women Who Will Inspire You on Your Journey to Healing

Library of Congress Control Number: 2010916615

Cover and Interior Graphic Design: Mike Baugher
Senior Editor: Jack Hopkins
Associate Editor: Nancy Newman
Compilation by Lisa Hardwick
Content Assistant and Proof Executive Assistant: Haley York
Photographers: Kaitlin Lampley, Kent Henderson, Michael Duhe, Tressa Martin

Table of Contents

Foreword: 8

Introduction: 10

Chapter 1:   13
Mind-Body-Spirit Connection To Wellness

Chapter 2:   59
I Don't Live Life, I Love Life

Chapter 3:   79
Beauty Is a Choice

Chapter 4:   121
Living in Laughter

Chapter 5:   155
The Beautiful Truth

About the Authors   179
Nancy Newman
Lisa Hardwick
Elaine Lemon
Robyn Podboy
Cindy Ray

Foreword

Imagine walking into a floral shop; you are immediately captivated by a mixture of vivid colors, and a scent that causes your brain to dance with excitement as you look at a most beautiful flower in front of you. Thinking of how fortunate you are to happen upon this most spectacular flower just after walking in, you are delightfully surprised - if not shocked - when you discover, just around the corner, yet another flower of a different type, that floods your senses with ecstasy-like feelings of pleasure. Then, this happens again, and again, and again with each new nook you explore in this floral heaven. You are in for a very similar experience with this book.

Each author, while the shape, size, color and scent, of their "flower" is different from the last – each unique in its own brilliant way - floods your senses with a message of hope and strength, in a way that only that particular author can.

Much like sitting at a large round table, surrounded by women full of love, compassion, warmth, wisdom and insight, the experience of reading this book leaves you with a feeling of a quiet confidence; an inner knowing, that no matter what you have endured in the past, what you might be dealing with now, or, what you might encounter in the future, you will be okay.

As you read each page, enjoy the feeling of having someone sitting next to you; a friend who, for that moment, is focused on nothing else in the world but you and your wellbeing. I don't suppose I have to tell you how soothing such a feeling is, or how much it inspires you to turn yet another page, then another, and another.

Read it, soak it in slowly, let the words and messages within fill you from the inside out, and know that each time you return, looking forward, once again, to that inner smile the wonderful stories within elicit in your heart and soul, that you can do so, anytime you choose, by allowing the stories to become a healthy part of your DNA, filling you with love and a sense of heightened purpose for the role you have in this beautiful world.

Dr. Clare Albright
Author of *Neurofeedback: Transforming Your Life with Brain Biofeedback*
www.DrClarity.com

Introduction

It is no mistake you are holding this book in your hands right now, at this very moment in your life, because this book is a part of YOUR personal journey to wholeness and your authentic self through messages of hope, healing and love.

It has been said that when the student is ready, the teacher will appear. This book contains the powerful personal stories and teachings from five diverse teachers, each from a unique perspective, which will forever change your thinking. As your thoughts change, your life experience will also change, and you will never be the same again.

NANCY NEWMAN

will familiarize you with the basics of the mind-body-spirit connection to wellness, and show how what you think and what you believe can have just as much if not more influence on your physical experience of life than genetics or luck! She believes your body is like Doppler radar communicating through your subconscious mind all your unresolved emotions which manifest in your body as symptoms and dis-ease. She gives you a four-step plan to healing and living your authentic life. Nancy offers the gifts of healing, loving yourself and peace within by sharing the tools which will allow you to create the life of your dreams!

LISA HARDWICK

will convey the importance of forgiveness – letting go of the pain. It is only the thoughts and feelings that you give your "stamp of approval" and say "YES!" to, that have the power to influence or direct any aspect of your beautiful life. Lisa encourages you to leave your hurtful and painful memories in the past where they belong and provides you with nine concrete steps to release those memories. By choosing to do so, you'll make your life happier, and life will take you somewhere good! Lisa leaves us this beautiful message: "As you embark on your journey towards survival and a happier life, please know that I, Lisa Hardwick, send forth my love, and wish you beautiful healing."

ELAINE LEMON

offers her lessons through metaphors which directly relate to her own personal life experiences. She tells us that authenticity is the only way to fully live life, and that Truth is revealed as you let go of the lies. Elaine teaches that when you decide to quit being a victim of your conditions by being accountable for your disappointments, you consciously choose a positive outcome. Your ego is a gift to you when it is a servant to your Spirit. Elaine feels that every single one of you has a beautiful purpose longing to be expressed which brings joy and abundance not only to yourself but also to many others. Her words of love will be a catalyst and inspiration to the discovery of your own inner essence, which is beyond beautiful.

ROBYN PODBOY

teaches you by her example that you have the power of CHOICE in how you live your life. She feels that she has learned most of her life lessons through laughter, and she will have you laughing from the very first page! For Robyn, laughter has been a crutch to lean on, a shield to hide behind, and a way to live her best life. Humor is the beginning of wisdom, and the best times in life are when you are laughing because this is when you are connected with your soul. Robyn urges us all to be authentic and make choices to support how healthy and happy you can be. Life was meant to be happy! What are you waiting for? Laugh!

CINDY RAY

shares the inspirational story of her journey back to love, which she feels began when she was "evicted from her life." Cindy dedicated her story to her late friend, Donna "Mac" McDonald. After Mac's, death, Cindy was determined to find answers so she could feel that living was better than dying, and so no one else would ever feel that dying was better than living. Her personal journey back to love took her through several painful experiences which will resonate with many of you. This is Cindy's story of her journey to find answers, and if it is your story, you are certain to find words of hope and help, and answers to your own painful doubts and fears.

Each one of the women in this book have been through some of life's roughest and most challenging experiences, but have emerged healed, whole and healthy! Their personal stories will have you laughing, crying, shaking your head in amazement – but through their incredible wisdom and love, they will show you the way to healing, hope, happiness, joy and peace.

Buckle your seat belt and get ready for an incredible ride – your journey to find wholeness! Say goodbye to your old ways of thinking and being. You are about to embark on the path to finding your authentic self. Have a safe journey. May we be the first to welcome the NEW YOU!

Nancy Newman

Dedicated to Dan, Jenni and London,
for your love and support.
You make my heart sing every day!

Chapter One
Mind-Body-Spirit Connection To Wellness

Chapter One

Mind-Body-Spirit Connection To Wellness
Listen To Your Body Talk!

A worldwide movement is challenging the long-held beliefs of the traditional medical world. That movement is the MIND-BODY-SPIRIT CONNECTION TO WELLNESS. No longer is it necessary to relegate your health challenges to merely genetics or bad luck, or your life experience to "luck of the draw"! There is now growing scientific evidence to support previous anecdotal evidence that what we think and what we believe can have just as much if not more influence on your physical experience of life than genetics or luck!

Wellness is beyond just physical health or dis-ease. Wellness is a state of being. Wellness is your experience of life and the challenges and lessons you are here to learn. Wellness has been described and defined in many ways.

I have defined wellness as: A state of being, reached through the process of making choices, either consciously or subconsciously, that affect the balance of your physical, mental, emotional and spiritual well-being.[1]

Eastern medicine has long embraced the mind-body-spirit connection to wellness and to the physical experience of life. European medicine joined the movement and incorporated the mind-body-spirit connection into their practice, and now it is becoming mainstream in America and is even being taught by traditional medical schools such as Dr. Andrew Weil's Integrative Medicine Clinic at the University of Arizona School of Medicine.

In America, one of the pioneers in this movement is Louise L. Hay, founder of Hay House Publishing and international best-selling author and speaker. Her first book, *Heal Your Body* (also known fondly as the "Little Blue Book"), was published in 1976, then revised and expanded in 1988. Louise was teaching the mind-body-spirit connection to wellness and the law of attraction over 30 years before *The Secret*[2] became a phenomenon!

Some individuals still believe that the mind-body-spirit connection falls solely within the purview of New Age Thought, and it is frequently relegated to the "woo-woo" category. Despite some detractors, recent scientific research by doctors and scientists such as Dr. Deepak Chopra, Dr. Bruce Lipton, Gregg Braden, Dr. Masaru Emoto, Dr. Andrew Weil and others demonstrates that science and physics have stepped into the equation and brought legitimacy to the belief. PBS, Discovery Channel, and other "mainstream" media have featured the concept and teachings.

Dr. Wayne Dyer, Dr. Bernie Siegel, Dr. Emmett Miller, Caroline Myss, Caroline Sutherland, Dr. Joan Borysenko, Denise Linn, Dr. Christiane Northrup, Dr. Mona Lisa Schulz, Esther and Jerry Hicks, and Dr. David Hamilton are just a few of the many other internationally-known authors and experts in their fields now teaching and writing about these concepts.

A Brief Overview of the Science

Dr. Deepak Chopra is a world-renowned authority in the field of mind-body healing, a best-selling author, the founder of the Chopra Center for Wellbeing and a former chief of staff for Boston Regional Medical Center. Heralded by *Time Magazine* as the "poet-prophet of alternative medicine," he is also the host of the popular weekly Wellness Radio program on Sirius/XM Stars. A global force in the field of human empowerment, Dr. Chopra is the prolific author of more than fifty-five books, including fourteen bestsellers on mind-

body health, quantum mechanics, spirituality, and peace.[3]

Dr. Chopra describes the mind-body connection as your "quantum mechanical body – the level at which your every thought is turned into physical reality." He continues by saying that "your body is a 3-D projection of your current state of mind. Your slightest shift of mood is picked up by every cell, which means that you do not think with your brain alone — all 50 trillion cells in your body actively share your thoughts. At the level of the quantum mechanical body, you are a constantly flowing river of intelligence. Correctly channeled, it has enormous power – the power to make us sick or well, depressed or joyful, sluggish or dynamic. The mind body connection is the gateway to unlimited creativity and happiness. Unfortunately, our society has not taught us how to use it."[4]

So, Dr. Chopra believes that we do not "think" with our brain alone, that the cells in our body actively share our thoughts! But can this be proven, in the laboratory, with actual cells?

Epigenetics, the new science of self-empowerment, is the subject of Dr. Bruce Lipton's groundbreaking book, *The Biology of Belief*. "Epigenetics, which literally means 'control above genetics,' profoundly changes our understanding of how life is controlled. In the last decade, epigenetic research has established that DNA blueprints passed down through our genes are not set in concrete at birth. Genes are not our destiny! Environmental influences, including nutrition, stress, and emotions, can modify those genes without changing their basic blueprint. "[5]

Imagine that! Dr. Lipton, a leading cellular biologist, proved through his research that not only can a cell function without a "brain" (by denucleation), but also, and perhaps more importantly, that a cell can be influenced by its environment (hostile or nurturing), and its DNA can be influenced by those cells surrounding it. Our genetic make-up is not our destiny.

New York Times best-selling author Gregg Braden is internationally renowned as a pioneer in bridging science and spirituality. Following a successful career as a Computer Geologist for Phillips

Petroleum during the 1970s energy crisis, he became a Senior Computer Systems Designer for Martin Marietta Defense Systems during the last years of the Cold War. In 1991 he was appointed the first Technical Operations Manager for Cisco Systems where he led the development of the global support team that assures the reliability of today's Internet.[6]

"Between 1993 and 2000, a series of groundbreaking experiments revealed dramatic evidence of a web of energy that connects everything in our lives and our world—the Divine Matrix. From the healing of our bodies, to the success of our careers, relationships, and the peace between nations, this new evidence demonstrates that we each hold the power to speak directly to the force that links all of creation.

Fact: The universe is made of a shared matrix of energy that underlies our Physical world.

Fact: Belief is a language that "speaks" to this matrix.

"Scientific evidence reveals that heart-based belief affects everything from the healing of our bodies to the atoms of our world. Is it possible that we're born with the power to reverse disease, create peace and abundance, and even change reality itself? As we face the greatest challenges of human history, these new discoveries suggest that we're about to find out!"[7]

So Gregg Braden believes that we each hold the power to speak directly to the force that connects all creation (the Matrix), and that "Belief" is a language that "speaks" to this matrix!

This is just a sampling of the many revelations that Dr. Chopra, Dr. Lipton and Mr. Braden have brought to the attention of the world! But how does this help the individual to make changes in their own life? If science has proven that the mind-body-spirit is connected and can be used for one's highest good, how can the average, every-day Joe learn these techniques and put this knowledge to their personal use?

My Story

I haven't always been the joyful, confident, successful, assertive, spirit-filled woman I am today at age 62. It has only been through a process of identifying those parts of myself that needed healing, embracing those parts, then "writing" a new story for myself that I have been able to transcend my past into peace and joy in the present!

My background, or at least parts of it, is probably similar in many respects to a lot of you reading this. Every person on the earth has challenges while walking their own unique path. My belief is that earth experience is like a "university." We all make an agreement before we come to the planet as to what lessons we want to learn, and we sign up for certain "classes."

I am sort of an all-or-nothing type of person. If I'm signing up for classes or workshops, I have a hard time limiting the scope. So I visualize being over on the other side, reading through the catalog of earth "classes" with my "advisor," and imagine my reactions to be something like this:

"Wow, Divorce I AND Divorce II? TWO classes in Divorce? Sign me up for both of those! Geez, you have several classes on Emotional Issues? Maybe I should make that my minor since I really have an interest in that! But which ones should I choose? Let's start with a class on anxiety disorder and one on panic attacks. The extended class on Depression is a must. Hmm, what else? Oh, I just HAVE to take post-traumatic stress syndrome AND just for fun, throw in the dissociative disorder group, too! Sexual abuse AND Rape? No way, you have each of them? I should learn a lot from those, so I'll do both. Weight issues? Well, I'll do it only if I can do the whole group up through morbid obesity. Maybe that should be my major since I can foresee taking a LOT of classes on that!"

And, so on. I must have signed up for just about every "class" that was available, and if there were advanced classes or extended classes, I most certainly signed up for those as well!

Some of the highlights of my unique path include being badly burned at age 18 months; loss of an infant sister when I was age six; several moves and changing schools (moved four times in three years and attended eight different schools in six years); the act of biting my arm for several years as a young child (while hiding in the closet or under the bed); emotional, physical and sexual abuse; incest; rape; two marriages and subsequent divorces; alcoholism in the family (both biological and through marriage); suicide attempts in the family (both biological and through marriage); periodic debt issues; business failures; bankruptcy; the loss of a baby and resulting hysterectomy; numerous medical issues and surgical procedures beginning at age three; sexual harassment in the workplace; extra-marital affairs; a near-death experience; quite a few automobile accidents (two of which were severe); history of weight issues (both under-eating and over-eating) beginning at age five going up to chronic clinical morbid obesity as an adult; diagnosed clinical depression (more than once); diagnosed panic attacks, panic disorder and anxiety disorder; diagnosed post-traumatic stress syndrome; diagnosed dissociative amnesia; and diagnosed depersonalization disorder.

In addition, for many years, I was a single mom with a young son receiving no child support. (I can remember going two and three days without eating, so the food we did have was available for him.) I have been fired or laid-off from more than one job. I've been on the brink of foreclosure of my house twice. And, like many others, I often experienced betrayal in countless ways by numerous people.

I'm sure that lots of readers have had one or more similar issues as those listed above. To be sure, mine has been a challenging path (as have the paths of many others in their own way). Reading through the highlights above, it would seem that I would be a mess, and, I'll admit that for a good portion of my life I was. But to meet me now, you would probably never guess any of those issues applied to me!

Growing up in Texas in the 1950's and 1960's certainly wasn't easy for a little girl with very different beliefs from those around her! I believed in equal rights (both racial and for women). I believed that we should help one another, not just have a "what's in it for me" attitude. I believed that everyone should be held accountable for

their actions. I believed in peace, not only within one's self, but as a goal for mankind. I believed that no one should be subjected to the tyranny and power of another. These were certainly not ideals which I was seeing demonstrated around me, nor were they shared by the majority of the people in my world!

In terms of spirituality and religion, the teachings of the churches of northeastern Texas (in the Bible belt) just did not resonate with me. I felt those teachings were fear-based, shame-based, guilt-inducing and certainly not love-based. I always felt that I could be closer to God by sitting outside under a tree than just sitting through a sermon filled with hatefulness and fear.

I was also very psychic and intuitive, which was believed to be something "of the Devil" according to the Bible. I was called evil and reviled by some people. I couldn't understand what all the fuss was about because I didn't realize that everyone didn't just "know" things.

Like many of you reading this, I was not safe from some of the males in my environment, both in my family and outside my family. Rather than effecting change with the perpetrators of verbal, physical and sexual abuse, I was taught to just "pull up my bootstraps and go on." My pleas for help were met with instructions to not cry and not make waves, just ignore what was happening and it would go away. So I learned not to complain, that I was on my own, and I particularly learned not to feel.

Since crying in particular was seen as a sign of weakness, I learned not to cry and not to feel any emotions. Remember the slogan on the commercial, "Never let them see you sweat"? My slogan was, "Never let them see you cry." I took pride in my stoicism and lack of visible emotion.

In fact, as mentioned before, I learned how to dissociate in threatening situations. The clinical term is dissociative amnesia and depersonalization disorder. The reality is that beginning when I was a child, in order to cope with the trauma I was experiencing, I would "slip out" of my conscious mind. That is a great way to not feel anything physically OR emotionally. But I paid a price for not being fully conscious. From the age of six to the age of eleven, I have two or three memories. That's all for that five-year period; the rest is a total blank. I can recall lots of things before age six, even memories of being a toddler, but very little between six and eleven (which is just opposite of most folks who don't remember much before age five).

During my adult life, I continued to experience the effects of the dissociative disorder in stressful or threatening situations (real or perceived) whenever I felt I had no escape, and I would slip into a dissociative episode. With the help of therapy and a lot of work and healing, the episodes have decreased in both intensity and frequency. As I have learned that I have a voice and that I can stand in my own power, the subconscious need to dissociate diminishes.

Another of my lessons from childhood was that women and blacks were the lowest rung on the ladder and were, therefore, accorded no rights or privileges whatsoever. Interestingly, one of the people in my world who loved me unconditionally was a black woman! Another was my grandmother. Two people, resting on the lowest rung of the ladder (as defined by the male hierarchy at that time), were the ones who showed me the most kindness, compassion, acceptance and unconditional love!

I was also taught that men were "the boss." They got to make all the decisions. They could engage in any behavior they wanted and never be held accountable. The experience of simply being female during that time taught me another lesson in not being valued. I felt defective somehow, and I didn't even know what I had done wrong!

By the time the mid-60's came along, I was really embracing the peace movement. I resonated with the songs by the folk singers like Peter, Paul & Mary, the Chad Mitchell Trio, and later with the words of singer songwriters such as John Lennon of the Beatles in songs like "Imagine." I admired Martin Luther King, Jr. and John F. Kennedy (unlike my family who were conservative Republicans). I longed to have peace in the world (and in MY world) and felt helpless to do anything about it. My adult self finds it incredibly sad

that here, 40 to 50 years later, all the folk songs and peace anthems are still relevant in our world of today. However, I no longer feel helpless in the pursuit of peace and take steps every day to bring peace to myself, others and the world.

I did not participate in the drugs or pot-smoking prevalent in the 1960's and early 1970's. In fact, I never smoked cigarettes or drank alcohol (except for about five memorable occasions!). But I did take the "free love" mantra to heart! My behavior during those years was very promiscuous and sometimes exposed me to great physical danger. I was simultaneously defiant and ashamed. Of course, I didn't have a clue that it was related to the sexual abuse I endured as a child, and again, just thought that I was defective somehow.

In my late teens, I became engaged to someone I had known for only three days. It all happened so fast, I didn't even know his last name! He wanted to get married, and it never occurred to me I could say no. Looking back, it was bizarre behavior on both our parts, but at the time it seemed so romantic – like a fairy tale! I soon discovered that he was very similar to those men of my childhood who thought power and fear were the methods to control others.

While married to my first husband, I had my near-death experience. This was a true turning point in my life. I had been pregnant, but it was a very rare abnormal pregnancy known as an abdominal pregnancy. The placenta and baby had slipped out of a hole in my uterus and had implanted in my abdomen, attaching to my intestines and other internal organs while still being connected to my uterus through the hole. This was prior to the use of ultrasound in early pregnancy, so it was thought I was either having a very large baby or perhaps a multiple birth.

When I was in my fourth month, the placenta detached and pulled out of the uterus, breaking the vacuum and causing the uterus to literally explode. I was told that it looked like a shotgun blast. Because of the rich, extensive vascular system that is created in the uterus during a pregnancy, when the veins were compromised, I actually bled out internally. By the time I reached the hospital, I had no pulse and no blood pressure, signs of clinical death. I won't go into the details of my near-death experience here except to say that every aspect of my life was forever changed.

It was only three months after the near-death experience that my second life-changing event occurred: a newborn baby boy found his way to me. This was the most wonderful gift I could have ever imagined. Our connection was (and is) that of a unique specialness to me transcending time and space.

In the course of the three-month period during which I lost my baby in the pregnancy along with the simultaneous near-death experience followed by adopting a newborn baby, I began to intensely research and study metaphysics, holistic health, Eastern medicine, Eastern spiritual philosophies, etc. attempting to find meaning for these things that had happened to me. I could not accept that it was all "just a fluke" or "just an accident." This was the beginning of what would turn into a life-long passion and ultimately a career in self-help, spirituality and holistic beliefs.

About five years after my son came into my life, my first husband and I divorced as I desired to protect him from his father's misguided attempts to control us. I also didn't want my son to grow up thinking this was how marriage, fatherhood and treating women should be practiced.

> { Most people are *doing the best they can,*
> given what they know and understand, including you.
> If they knew more and were aware of more,
> they would *do things differently.* }
> ~ Louise Hay

I realize now that my first husband was merely living life and being married as he had seen modeled to him as a child. He was only doing what he knew how to do. During our time together, he never found an opportunity to do things differently. I hope he has been able to do so after we parted ways.

Through my classes and studies in Sacred Contracts by Caroline Myss, I have come to believe that he and I had a sacred contract with each other to learn a life lesson and/or a Soul lesson. I believe that one of my lessons with him was to have the opportunity to do what I was most terrified of doing: leaving him, claiming my power and standing up for myself. I believed physical harm and death were very real possibilities. I wasn't worried about the actual experience of death, after all I had already done that once before! My fear was that my dying would leave my young son alone to be raised by his father.

Utilizing tools I have learned, I have now forgiven my former husband and his actions toward me and our son. I'm actually thankful for our time together and the resulting lessons I learned and the skills I developed.

Soon after my first divorce, my research and study led me to Louise Hay and her book, *You Can Heal Your Life*. In this book Louise explains how our beliefs and ideas about ourselves are often the cause of our emotional problems and physical maladies and how, by using certain tools, we can change our thinking and our lives for the better. Her practical, easy-to-understand philosophy certainly resonated within me. I had never read anything like that, yet it seemed so "familiar" to me.

Not long after I found Louise Hay and the mind-body connection, I was diagnosed for the first time with vaginal Level 3 dysplasia (the last stage before Stage I cancer) as a result of my mother being given DES[8] when she was pregnant with me. My doctor at the time advised surgical intervention as he had never seen it "spontaneously" just go away. However, by using Louise Hay's philosophies and exercises, I was able to reverse and clear the dysplasia without medical or surgical intervention.

With the tools taught by Louise, I identified the emotional thought pattern(s) and beliefs that contributed to my body accepting this state of dis-ease. The same condition has returned twice since that time, giving me additional opportunities for further healing. I feel that all our challenges are gifts to help identify those areas in our life and our subconscious that need attention and healing.

After each of my divorces, I used many coping strategies to numb myself to the challenges in my life. My personal favorite coping strategies were working too much, volunteering too much and eating too much. By unknowingly "anesthetizing" myself with these coping mechanisms, I was depriving my son (and me) of our precious time together. I justified the time away by telling myself I was doing important things, or that I was working so much to be able to provide "things" for him. It wasn't until after he was grown and gone that I realized the true cost paid and how my behavior affected him.

> If I made you feel second best,
> *I am sorry, I was blind.*
> You were always on my mind.
>
> You were always on my mind.
>
> ~Willie Nelson
> *"You Were Always on My Mind"*

A book I highly recommend to parents is, *To a Child LOVE is Spelled T-I-M-E* by Mac Anderson and Lance Wubbels[9], who write that sometimes we all need reminding that, "the most important things in life aren't things." I certainly wish I had known this thirty years ago.

Besides being physically unavailable to him for several years, when I went into my severe chronic depressive state in the early to mid-1990's, I was emotionally unavailable to him as well. Of all the things in my life that I wish I could change, it would be spending more time with him and being there for him. I felt terrible guilt for many years until I learned to forgive myself. I can't change those years, but I can do better about our time in the future, and do what I can to help others "know better" now, while there's still time to implement change.

{
I did then what I knew how to do.
Now that I know better, *I do better.*

~ Maya Angelou
}

Throughout the years since I discovered Louise Hay and her philosophy, I have shared her principles with anyone who would listen! (And, I imagine, some who didn't WANT to listen!) After nearly 30 years of loving Louise and embracing her philosophy, it was my honor to become a Licensed Heal Your Life® Workshop Leader/Teacher in September, 2010. I continued with advanced training and in February, 2011, obtained my license as a Heal Your Life® Coach. I know absolutely that I am in service to Spirit when I can see the positive changes in students and clients by sharing these principles developed by Louise.

Along the way, I also trained in other healing modalities such as Reflexology and energy work becoming a certified Reiki Master.[10] In addition, I am a registered Master Toe Reader.

The system and practice of Toe Reading as a healing discipline was developed by KC Miller, the founder of the Southwest Institute of Healing Arts. KC was a student of Louise Hay and practiced as a Reflexologist. Through thousands of clients over the years, she noticed that similar characteristics on the feet and toes went along with similar stories from the clients possessing those toes! From that, she developed the system of Toe Reading.[11]

Toe Readers believe that a person's beliefs and past experiences are imprinted holographically in the toes and feet. A person's life story is literally "written" in their toes. It is a Toe Reader's job to interpret the signs and help the person understand what their body is trying to communicate to them through metaphors. A Toe Reader can then assist the person to facilitate change if a belief isn't working in their life. Toe Readers consider themselves Soul (Sole) Coaches.

I trained with KC Miller, Cheryl Speen and Kaye Coleman at the Southwest Institute of Healing Arts through the various certification levels of Toe Reading until receiving the highest designation of Master Toe Reader. I've always found that being a Toe Reader has helped me with my teaching of Louise Hay, and being a student of Louise Hay has helped me with my Toe Reading! Both healing modalities rely on the premise of the mind-body-spirit connection to wellness.

I have used Louise Hay's philosophies in all aspects of my life to identify those areas needing healing or needing additional healing, to change my circumstances, to forgive those I needed to forgive (including myself), to change my relationship with money, to lose weight – in short, just about my whole experience of life has been affected by knowing the principles of Louise Hay! My life was further enhanced when I learned Toe Reading.

As I was attending my training to be a Louise Hay Licensed Heal Your Life® Workshop Leader/Teacher, each participant had to re-write our "story." In my old story, one of my beliefs was that no one wanted to listen to what I had to say. My new story affirmed that I was "a writer, teacher and healer who creates and shares programs all over the world that bring joy, healing and peace to others."

At the time, I had no idea how my new story would materialize. But I believed with all my heart that it was true, and I affirmed my new "reality" to myself every day. Since you are reading this, you know that my new story has indeed become REALITY! You are holding that reality in your hands right now.

I am passionate about teaching the mind-body-spirit connection to wellness, so let's get started! You've learned the basics of the science behind it, you've heard how I've used it to make changes in my life and wellness, now let's learn how to put it to practical use to facilitate the change YOU desire in YOUR own personal experience of life and wellness.

Become a Co-Creator of Your Life Experience

We all depend on Doppler radar to let us know when bad weather is on the way. What if we had our own personal Doppler radar to let us know what is going on in our subconscious mind; and further, what if we were able to use that knowledge to our advantage?

Just as Doppler radar can let us know a snow storm or rain is on the way, our bodies are like Doppler radar communicating to us what is going on in our subconscious mind and what unresolved emotions we have such as anger, resentment, criticism, fear, grief, etc. These unresolved emotions manifest in our bodies as symptoms and dis-ease.

When we face challenges in our health, for example, most of us immediately think how unlucky we are. That it is just a stroke of bad luck, luck of the draw or even genetics that we broke our ankle, needed a root canal, got laryngitis, got a bladder infection, got cancer, got a zit, hit our elbow resulting in a bruise, have a sore shoulder, have an aching back, etc.

Actually, these are all examples of our body talking to us, trying to communicate to us that we are rebelling against "authority" in our life and feeling inflexibility and guilt over receiving pleasure (broken ankle); that we are experiencing long-standing indecision (root canal); that we are resentful and don't feel we "have a voice" (laryngitis); that we are "pissed off" (bladder infection); that we have a deep grief or possibly still carrying around long-standing hurts and resentment that are "eating away" at us (cancer); that we feel anger and it is "oozing out" (acne); that we are scared about changing directions and are punishing ourselves in some way for the decision or indecision (bruised elbow); that we feel resentment at the "burdens we are carrying" (sore shoulder); or, that we are frightened about our finances (aching lower back), and so on.

Eye problems? Is there something you don't want to "see"? Ear problems? Is there something you don't want to "hear"? Are you getting the hang of this yet? These are all examples of our body talking to us.[12] This is the language our body uses to communicate to us that something is amiss in our world! Seem simple? That's because it IS simple. It's just a language that we can easily learn.

Some of you may be asking: Why would we even want or need to learn this new "language"? The answer is that if we are feeling fear, anger, guilt, resentment, etc., these emotions and the resulting thought patterns will create undesirable situations in our life and/or physical symptoms or disease in our bodies! How good would it feel to know you have the power to create loving, nurturing situations in your life and vibrant health in your body instead?

In 1984 the groundbreaking book by Louise Hay, *You Can Heal Your Life*, was first published and has since been translated into 29 different languages selling over 35 million copies world-wide, reaching the *New York Times* bestseller list and remaining there for 13 consecutive weeks. Why? Because her concepts and philosophies offer real help and truth, and are presented in an easy-to-understand format.

Louise's key message in this powerful work is: "If we are willing to do the mental work, almost anything can be healed." Louise explains how limiting beliefs and ideas are often the cause of illness, and how you can change your thinking thereby improving the quality of your life!

What physical symptoms and/or ailments are you experiencing in your life? These are the emotions and thoughts that your body is trying to communicate to you. Don't ignore this very valuable body Doppler radar that is at your disposal! Your body won't give up trying to talk to you. It will keep giving you more and more and more severe symptoms and/or unpleasant life situations until it gets your attention. Give it your attention now. Learn the language of your body. Listen to your body talk!

Consistent Thinking Patterns and Beliefs Create Our Experiences

You've been exposed to the basics of listening to your body talk, and you understand the message. Now what? Just knowing doesn't facilitate change. Just looking up the meanings of your physical symptoms and dis-ease in *You can Heal Your Life* or *Heal Your Body* doesn't make your broken ankle better, or the emotional belief and thought pattern that allowed it to manifest to disappear without some resulting work on your part. YOU need to actually do the work, not just read about it!

One of the first steps is to learn how to do affirmations. Affirmations absolutely can change your life. But again, just doing an affirmation and changing one aspect of your life or physical health isn't the solution. It is merely addressing a symptom. It is not addressing the root cause. Until you HEAL the underlying cause, your symptoms or pattern in life will return, or other symptoms and dis-ease or pattern in life that result from the same or similar thought pattern will appear in its place.

Our consistent thinking patterns and beliefs create our experiences. Therefore, by releasing some of these thinking patterns and beliefs that are contributing to an undesirable experience of health or life experience, we can change our experiences.

As identified by Louise Hay, the four main mental thought patterns that cause the most dis-ease in the body are: Criticism, Resentment, Fear and Guilt. She calls these the "Big Four." Further, resentment is, in reality, anger that has been stuffed down. Louise stated recently that The Big Four can really be narrowed down to just two: Fear and Anger.

Anger can show up as impatience, irritation, frustration, criticism, resentment, jealousy or bitterness. Fear could be tension, anxiety, nervousness, worry, doubt, feeling not good enough or unworthiness. As has been stated, the feeling of not being good enough is nearly universal.

Do any of these mental thought patterns or feelings show up in your life? No matter what the problem is, our experiences are just outer effects of inner thoughts and beliefs, from a refusal to let go and come into the present moment.

> It's only a thought and
> *a thought can be changed.*
> ~ Louise Hay

The point of power to change our thinking is right now. In this very moment. If we are the product of our past thoughts and beliefs, then it follows that we will be the product of our thoughts and beliefs from this moment forward.

What type of life do you want to create? Are your thoughts conducive to creating that type of life? Doesn't it feel better to think about love, peace, joy and self-approval than criticism, anger, resentment and guilt? The best gift you will ever give yourself is the gift of healing, loving yourself and discovering peace within.

Healing, Loving Yourself and Discovering Peace Within

Healing, loving yourself and discovering peace within is not an instantaneous process. Although some are able to immediately achieve paradigm shifts in their thinking, for most it is an on-going process. Even if a seemingly "instantaneous" shift occurs, situations will occur in your life to "test" this new way of thinking. For some, the "testing" may continue for years.

Don't be discouraged! You didn't learn to walk, ice skate or ride a bike without taking a few falls, and it will be no different with new ways of thinking and being. The solution is to get right back up, FORGIVE YOURSELF and go on.

> *To forgive* is the highest,
> most beautiful form of love.
>
> In return, you will receive
> untold *peace and happiness.*
>
> ~ Robert Mueller

Forgiveness is also an expression of your Spirit and your connection with the Divine. One of the most famous quotes on forgiveness is by Alexander Pope: "To err is human, to forgive, divine." Let me be clear: Forgiveness is NOT condoning hurtful behavior or "letting someone off the hook." Forgiveness is also not pushing away thoughts of what happened and just moving on. This is only burying the hurt, fear, rage, guilt, etc. inside your spirit deeper and deeper. Then the only way it can come to the surface is through attracting similar situations into your life in a subconscious attempt to "resolve" the original situation, or through painful and sometimes life-threatening bodily symptoms and diseases. We have to move through the feelings, not around them!

> *Forgiveness* does not change the past,
> but it does enlarge *the future.*
>
> ~ Paul Boese

Many of us attempt to avoid feeling those original feelings at a deep, core level. We just push those thoughts away and try to forget. Some of us will try to "swallow" those feelings through over-eating. Some of us will try to "obscure" the feelings through smoking tobacco or other substances. Some of us will try to "forget" those feelings through self-medication with pills, powders and/or alcohol. Some of us will try to "overcome" those feelings through trying to "over-power" others with manipulation and control. Some of us will try to "push away" the feelings through excessive socially-acceptable obsessive behaviors such as exercise, work, involvement in organizations, churches or volunteer work.

But none of these behaviors brings long-term relief. They are only a temporary "fix" and will require increasing intensity to keep the feelings at bay. All the while, we "think" we are dealing with it just fine! That is our ego, our conscious mind talking. Our bodies may be telling us a different story but most of us will just chalk it up to bad luck, genetics, getting chilled, the thought of "it's going around," or any one of a number of coping strategies that are actually denial of what is really happening.

Some of the more severe symptoms and dis-eases may take decades to fully develop. Wouldn't you rather learn how to deal with your feelings now without having a life-threatening challenge to deal with at the same time? Of course, you would. But lots of us are in denial that "it could happen to me," and a lot of us believe that we have no part in our experience of life and manifestation of physical symptoms and dis-ease. So most of us will do nothing about learning to deal with our feelings until there's a life-threatening situation in our life.

I'm inviting you to deal with your feelings and practice forgiveness NOW! Don't wait until you have to undergo drastic medical intervention and are experiencing panic and fear, then have to deal with those buried feelings at the same time! Do it now while you can put all your focus on healing buried feelings.

{
To forgive is to set a prisoner *free*
and discover that prisoner was *you*.
~ Lewis B. Smedes
}

I would like to make absolutely crystal clear that the mind-body-spirit approach to wellness does NOT advocate shunning traditional medicine and healing techniques. Instead, moving toward wellness by integrating traditional with alternative healing is the choice of many. If you are facing a life-threatening situation, you must explore all

avenues open to you. These can include any one or a combination of cutting-edge conventional medical techniques offered by Western medicine; nutritional therapies; Eastern medical techniques; holistic healing techniques; psychiatric therapy; yoga, acupuncture, chiropractic, hypnosis, meditation, Reiki, reflexology or other alternative therapies in an integrative manner.

In fact, there are medical practices all over the United States that offer both traditional and complementary healing methods in an integrative, holistic approach to treatment. The Cancer Treatment Centers of America, with sites around the country, is an example of this approach.[13] Of course, as mentioned previously, this methodology is much more common in other parts of the world.

Holistic is not another example of "woo-woo" as some may think. Holistic very simply means that all aspects of your life, of your being, are equally important. A holistic approach to your life means that your wellness is a balance of your emotional, physical, and spiritual needs – in other words, your mind, body and spirit connection to wellness! Remember my definition of wellness way back at the beginning? "A state of being, reached through the process of making choices, either consciously or subconsciously, that affect the balance of your physical, mental, emotional and spiritual well-being."

A word of caution is in order. Sometimes, after learning the power of our mind and how we can create our experience of life and wellness, a person will manifest dis-ease or a physical symptom, or encounter a challenging situation, then feel as if they have failed! After all, if THEY created this, then they haven't fully learned their lesson. While it is true that their thoughts have contributed to create this situation, this does not indicate FAILURE!

Rather, a challenging situation or physical experience in your life should be considered a GIFT! Your subconscious is illuminating an area in your life that needs some attention and healing. It is a wonderful gift! Be grateful, bless and thank your body and subconscious for the gift of awareness so you can change your thoughts!

Frequently, I hear from my clients and students: "But why have I gotten this condition BACK again? I did everything I was supposed to do. I worked really hard to heal it the FIRST time!"

These are valid questions. To answer, I will use myself as an example. I mentioned earlier that I had manifested vaginal cellular dysplasia three times! I had cleared it initially with lots of healing work, then it came back not once but two more times! What the heck went wrong? I had worked really hard on healing and forgiveness surrounding the abuse and rape issues. (By the way, I'm hoping that by this time you have connected the dots between the abuse and rape, and the location of my symptoms and dis-ease!)

So what was going on? Why was the dis-ease returning again and again? Upon reflection, I realized that I had not FULLY healed the wounds and trauma because I was able to heal only that which I WAS READY TO HEAL at the time! As I got stronger, new layers of areas needing healing were brought to my attention through my body talking to me!

I have heard healing described as going up a spiral staircase. We have an experience in our life, work to heal it, and move up the staircase. But eventually, we come back around to the same lesson, the difference being, this time, you are experiencing the lesson and healing at a higher level. You are now ready to continue the healing. As you go up the staircase, and come around each time, the lesson will be easier and less painful to heal.

Who knows, I might manifest the dysplasia again. But if so, I will view it as a gift from my subconscious and my body that I am now stronger and ready to heal even more painful areas!

You Are "Enough"

Loving, approving and accepting ourselves just the way we are is so crucial to our well being that not enough can be written about it, not enough reminding can be done about it, and not enough work can be done with it! According to Louise Hay, the innermost belief for

everyone she's worked with is the belief of not being good enough! She has written that everyone she knows or has worked with is suffering from some degree of self-hatred or guilt. Thoughts of "I'm not good enough, I don't deserve this, or I don't do enough" are common complaints she hears. Likewise, these are the most common statements I hear as well in my workshops and in private sessions.

But for whom are you not good enough? And by whose standards? I don't believe that the Universe makes unnecessary or imperfect people. We are each exactly where we are meant to be on our paths. YOU ARE ENOUGH!

> { Most people don't think they're enough of what they *already are.* }
> ~ Alan Cohen

Hmmm... let's ponder this for a second. "Most people don't think they're enough of what they already are." That's true, you know.

In the holistic field, it is said that everything we'll ever need we already have, and that everything we'll ever need to know we already know.

So, that would mean the statement is true that we are already "enough" of everything we already need to be. But for most of us, we don't "think" we are. So the reality already "is," it is only our "perception" that isn't! Whoa, that's heavy, huh? You might need to re-read these last three paragraphs a few times for this to sink in and make sense!

I can hear some of you protesting, "But that's not true. I want to be an engineer. I won't be 'enough' without a college education to get a degree in engineering." Well, perhaps, depending on our chosen field of endeavor, we might need to experience higher learning for specific training in a certain profession or trade. But the desire for

additional education doesn't change the person we are inside. It doesn't change the reality of who "we" really are inside.

"We" are always "enough" whether we have a college degree or not, whether we have a high school diploma or not, whether we are rich or poor, drive a VW or a Mercedes. It doesn't matter. What we do in life, or what we have in life is not what matters or determines whether or not we are "enough."

"We" are all good enough, smart enough, successful enough, free enough, pretty enough, handsome enough, rich enough, thin enough -- we are ENOUGH. But we spend most of our lives trying to be more. Trying to get smarter, prettier, richer, thinner -- when it's INSIDE that matters. And, inside we are all the same, and we all are ENOUGH!

So, the next time you are fretting over whatever it is that you don't have enough of, or you think that you don't measure up in some respect, remember that you already are ENOUGH. You just don't think you are. It's what's inside that counts.

No matter what area of your life is challenged, whether it is poor health, lack of abundance, yet another relationship that didn't work out, an unfulfilling job – the main thing that needs work is LOVING THE SELF! The secret to positive change in every area of your life is loving and approving of yourself exactly as you are! YOU ARE ENOUGH! Believe it. Live it.

Now, I can just hear your thought: "But how do I do that? How do I believe it?" One of the ways is affirmations; another is mirror work. And, I'm going to teach you the basics of both!

Affirmations

What are these mysterious things called affirmations anyway, and why would we want to do them? To some, I'm sure that sounds like that "woo-woo" stuff again!

Affirmations are simply replacing a negative, unnecessary thought or

pattern that is no longer useful for us, or which is creating a physical symptom or disease, with a new positive thought that will bring healthier, more positive experiences and people into our lives. Now, that isn't so mysterious or "woo-woo" is it?

Each of us carry around many beliefs about ourselves, about others, and about the world. Some of these beliefs no longer serve us but we hang onto them because they are safe, comfortable, and/or familiar.

A belief is an idea or thought that we have heard or read, then think it so often that we accept it as truth. The reality may be totally different than our "belief." But what we think about ourselves and the world becomes true for us. Our thoughts and statements become our "beliefs," which create our experience in either a positive or a negative way.

> {
> An *affirmation* is any
> statement that we make
> – whether positive or negative.
> ~ Louise Hay
> }

We can choose to live a joyous, hopeful, loving life or we can choose to live a life filled with pain, suffering and sorrow, because our subconscious accepts what we choose to believe. But whatever your beliefs may be about the world and yourself, remember that they are just thoughts, and thoughts can be changed.

A lot of us have come from backgrounds of verbal and sexual abuse, incest, rape, harsh judgment and criticism, severe corporal punishment, etc. These types of experiences, particularly in childhood, almost always lead to feelings and beliefs of unworthiness and self-hatred. We can be very unforgiving of ourselves and inflict self-punishment day after day in various ways thereby continuing the original "hurt."

Falls, broken bones, cuts, bruises – all of these can be ways we punish ourselves by hurting ourselves physically. Manifesting dis-ease or other painful physical symptoms are also ways we can punish or "hurt" ourselves by experiencing physical pain.

Another common way to punish ourselves for the past is with addictive behavior: We overeat, drink, act out compulsive sexual behavior, gamble too much, smoke cigarettes, create abusive love relationships, take legal and illegal pills and other substances, spend money that we don't have, work too much, become overly involved in church or volunteer activities, or any one of a myriad of compulsive behaviors and substances which numb ourselves to the feelings of unworthiness and self-hatred. Some of these ways are socially acceptable and/or legal, some are not. Engaging in dangerous or illegal activities is an even deeper level of self-punishment.

Do you believe the world is an unsafe place with people and situations waiting to get at you or hurt you? If so, that belief will become your reality and you will adopt coping strategies, which can include addictions, to try to counteract these feelings and beliefs. This belief can trigger your "flight or fight" response and create a constant source of stress for you mentally and physically. I have experienced this on a personal level and through the experiences of my clients.

Are you ready to let go of beliefs and behaviors that don't support and nurture you? It's not enough to simply "want" to let go, you must be willing to release the NEED as well.

For example, if your addictive behavior is overeating, just affirming that "I eat healthy foods that nurture and make my body whole," is not going to totally overcome the need to overeat. It will help you eat healthier foods, but you can still overeat! You aren't releasing the need for the addiction to the behavior of "overeating."

Your thoughts must be reprogrammed to know that the past is over and can't be changed. Begin by affirming: "I am willing to release the need for overeating in my life. I release it now and trust in the

process of life to meet my needs." (If overeating isn't your behavior, you can replace overeating in that affirmation with your behavior of choice!)

Okay, now that you have affirmed that you are willing to release the need for your behavior, or your physical dis-ease or symptom, or a life situation that is not bringing you pleasure and joy, what now? How do we attract these desired manifestations into our lives?

Creating Affirmations That Work

In Louise Hay's book, *The Power is Within You*, and in Dr. Patricia Crane's best-seller, *Ordering From the Cosmic Kitchen: The Essential Guide to Powerful, Nourishing Affirmations*, the analogy is made that when we put our desires out to the Universe, it is like putting in an order to the Cosmic Kitchen where the Cosmic Chef is just waiting to receive and fulfill our orders. Don't you just love that analogy? I do, too!

I believe that if your affirmations aren't manifesting the new experiences you desire into your life, it may be that you are unknowingly ordering your "steak" from the Cosmic Kitchen "rare," when you really want "well done"! Evidently, there must be some rules we need to learn!

In *Ordering From the Cosmic Kitchen*, Dr. Crane teaches eight principles to putting in your order. As presented by Dr. Crane, these principles are:

1. Decide what you want.
2. Make your orders positive, present tense and personal.
3. Use enthusiastic words.
4. Let go of your time line and trust Cosmic timing.
5. Let the Cosmic Chef prepare your order, stay out of the kitchen.
6. Find balance between action and allowing.
7. Believe that you deserve a wonderful life.
8. Feel gratitude for your orders coming in miraculous ways.

In addition, your subconscious has no sense of humor and takes things literally. For example, if you were to say, "I'm not going to eat ice cream anymore," your subconscious doesn't grasp the nuances of the "not going to" or "any more." It hears the literal statement "eat ice cream" and proceeds to give you cravings for ice cream! The more you affirm that you are not going to eat ice cream any more, the more you crave it!

Perhaps the flu or a cold is going around your family or your workplace, and you are feeling the initial sore throat, sniffles or body aches. If you say to yourself, "I'm NOT going to get sick," what happens? I suspect that more often than not, you get that cold or the flu anyway! What's going on? Again, your subconscious isn't hearing "not." It hears, "get sick."

There are many examples of unknowingly putting in a mistaken order with the Cosmic Kitchen and not manifesting what you desire. For example, you may affirm, "I'm going to get a new job," or "I'm going to find the love of my life." Phrasing your affirmations in this way is putting it off in the future. Your desired result is being programmed to be out there at some point in the future. If you keep repeating that affirmation, it will simply keep putting your desired result just beyond your reach.

Instead, you could affirm, "I am loving my new job and my new co-workers." Or, if you are hoping for a new life companion, how about, "I enjoy the company of my like-minded companion who is treating me with love and respect"? Don't those statements feel better?

The more you practice, the easier putting in your order to the Cosmic Kitchen starts to become. So, what are we waiting for? Let's start practicing!

Why don't we begin with health, one of my favorite areas! If your current belief is that "I don't heal well," you could affirm, "My body heals easily and quickly." For a belief of "My back always hurts," your affirmation could be, "Everyone in my life supports me and gives me unconditional love for my success." If you are constantly

repeating "I always get sick," or "I get a cold every winter," a more supportive thought would be: "Every cell in my body is constantly vibrating with energy and good health! "

Let's try some others. What about emotions? Belief: "I'm constantly nervous and experience anxiety all the time." Affirmation: "I trust in the process of life. I choose love, joy and freedom. I open my heart and allow wonderful things to flow into my life." Belief: "Getting old scares me." Affirmation: "My life is full of joy. I am a perfect age. I have an abundance of time to complete what I want to do." Belief: "I feel like a failure," or "I AM a failure." Affirmation: "I am proud of all I have accomplished. I am a valuable human being. I love and forgive myself for any past mistakes. " Belief: "I'm scared to be alone." Affirmation: "I give out love and love is returned to me multiplied. I am my own best friend and cheerleader. I am safe."

Are you experiencing challenges with money and abundance? That's a big one for many people right now with the current economy! Belief: "I'm never able to save money." Affirmation: "I am blessed with overflowing abundance which provides for all my wants and needs including a lavish savings account." Belief: "I don't make enough money." Affirmation: "My income is constantly increasing because I am deserving of abundance and joy." Belief: "I have a bad credit rating." Affirmation: "My credit rating improves daily." Belief: "I can't save for retirement." Affirmation: "I now create great wealth which allows me to joyfully save for my retirement." Belief: "I can't pay my bills." Affirmation: "I lovingly pay all my bills on time as I know abundance flows freely through me."

Have you experienced challenges in relationships? See if any of these beliefs resonate with you, then try the new affirmation! Belief: "Love always ends. Love is for everybody else, not for me." Affirmation: "I deserve to be loved and believe that love is eternal. I rejoice in the love I encounter every day." Belief: "If I'm in a relationship, everything has to be done their way." Affirmation: "My relationship is filled with peaceful, loving interactions which empower both partners." Belief: "I'm terrified of love." Affirmation: "I give myself permission to be greater than my fears. I attract my perfect partner. I am safe." Belief: "Everyone in my life always leaves me," or "Everybody always betrays me." Affirmation: "I deserve a long-lasting, fully committed relationship. I forgive and totally release my past. I welcome love into my wonderful new life." Belief: "I am not good enough," or "I am defective." Affirmation: "I am a perfect and valuable child of the Universe. I love myself just the way I am. I honor the best parts of myself and share them with others. I am MORE than enough."

Just to really get you into the groove, here are more affirmations by Dr. Patricia Crane from her book, *Ordering From the Cosmic Kitchen.* At this point, I'm confident that you'll be able to fill in the negative thought pattern just by reading the positive affirmation!

"I am deserving of a wonderful life. I now consciously create the life of my dreams! I easily create the ideal food and exercise plan so I achieve my ideal weight. I receive an abundance of love from my friends and family. I love and approve of myself. I am always doing the best I can. I am healthy, wealthy and wise. My income is constantly increasing. I'm having a love affair with life! I am delighted to be using my talents and abilities in my ideal career position. I now know and follow the Divine Plan for my life. I trust my Inner Wisdom, knowing that all the answers are within me."[14]

Wow, don't you feel uplifted by just reading all these positive affirmations? Can't you FEEL the difference inside with just the possibility that these could be true for you?

It is not necessary that you accept the affirmation as true at this point. In fact, you probably won't have any faith in it at all! My guess is that you may even be thinking that it is the craziest thing you've ever heard! But that's because it is not yet your belief, and you are working to change your belief.

Another way to put this is that when the "vibration" of what you desire exactly matches the "vibration" of your belief, what you desire will manifest.

What does this mean? Stated yet another way, when your belief is

not really what you are desiring, your desired manifestation won't appear. In other words, your conscious thought or desire is not in coherence with your subconscious belief.

When I am working on changing a belief with a new affirmation, I type it out on a piece of paper, cut it to size and tape it to the computer monitor both at home and at work. (Sticky notes work great as well.) Each time my eyes pass over the note, I read it to myself. Between the computer at work, and the computer at home, I am reading this new affirmation probably several hundred times a day.

By this one step alone, within a couple of months, the new belief is not sounding so crazy or foreign. It is feeling more comfortable. Eventually, this new thought is incorporated into that tape that plays in your head, and it becomes your new belief. Then your new belief creates new, more desirable situations in your life.

If your old belief was one that was manifesting in a physical symptom or illness, that symptom or illness will begin to abate when your new belief takes hold. Your body doesn't need to communicate to you any longer with that dis-ease or symptom because your new belief is being accepted as true for you.

Try to add some other spots in which to see your new affirmation, too. Instead of only putting your new affirmation on your computer, you could try also putting it in numerous places where you'll be sure to see it several times a day. How about on the refrigerator, the mirror in the bathroom, the phone, the hand lotion bottle, above the kitchen sink, your wallet, on the remote control – the location doesn't matter as long as it is something that you will see several times a day. The more you will see it, the better.

I've had some clients tell me that they are faithfully doing their affirmations, we've determined the affirmation is worded properly, but the things they are trying to manifest just don't seem to be happening. What's going on? As I mentioned previously, the vibration of your conscious thought needs to match the vibration of your desired result. If we are just starting to put the vibration out there, we can compare it to planting a seed in the garden – in this case, it is the garden of your subconscious!

When you plant a sunflower seed in your garden, it doesn't immediately spring forth as a fully grown sunflower reaching up to the heavens! Neither does your affirmation instantaneously manifest your new belief. The amount of time it takes for your new belief to completely "sprout" is the amount of time it takes for the fertile soil of your subconscious to fully embrace and accept the change. Or, as stated earlier, the amount of time it takes for your conscious vibration to totally match with your subconscious vibration.

There are numerous books on affirmations, but my personal favorites are Dr. Patricia Crane's *Ordering From the Cosmic Kitchen*, and any of the ones by Louise Hay. I invite you to explore their teachings in further depth. [15]

{ *Affirmations* ... they can become *a way of life!* }

Mirror Work

Mirror work is also a way of affirming to your subconscious, which Louise Hay and others believe is absolutely essential to healing and manifesting your desires.

I'm not gonna lie to you. For most of us, mirror work is extremely difficult in the beginning. For one thing, many have avoided even looking in mirrors unless absolutely necessary. We don't REALLY look at ourselves, or if we do, it is with criticism of what we see. Some people even hang their mirrors so the reflection is only from the neck down.

The first time I was asked to look in a mirror to do mirror work, I

was mortified! I was certain that the other people in the workshop would think I actually liked looking at myself, and what a lie that was! After all, I was fat and ugly, and my belief was that everyone else saw that as well. I absolutely could NOT look myself in the eye, much less say out loud that I loved myself. Then a strange thing happened. Shockingly, I heard nervous laughter from some in the workshop and sobbing from others! A couple of people actually bolted from the room, unable to even pick up their mirror. Could it be that these other people, who I thought were really attractive, did not like their reflection either? What a revelation!

For me, it took several weeks of daily practice before I could actually look deep into my own eyes, to speak out loud, and even longer to really mean what I said. Now, I love doing mirror work, even in front of others when I'm leading a workshop!

When doing mirror work at workshops I facilitate, I notice that most of the people immediately fluff their hair, or wipe something imaginary off their chin, women might check their lipstick or see if there's something in their teeth. All the while, we are usually thinking critical thoughts, thoughts of non-acceptance of what is, thoughts of how something could or should be better.

As I've learned in my healing journey, loving ourselves means never being critical of ourselves for any reason. Ever. Let me say that again. Loving yourself means that you never criticize yourself for any reason, ever. By being critical of ourselves, we lock ourselves into the very pattern we're trying to change.

Here's an experiment for you: For a whole week, at least seven full days, try approving of yourself and see what happens. For example, if you finish a large project that you've been putting off, congratulate yourself; tell yourself how wonderful you are for completing that project. When you go to the dentist to get your teeth cleaned, tell yourself what a good thing you've done for yourself. Find things that you can compliment yourself about.

You've most likely been criticizing yourself for years. Has it worked? Has criticism of yourself changed your life for the better? Or, as Dr. Phil frequently says, "How's that been workin' for ya?"

If you are experiencing physical ailments, disease and/or lack in your life, I suspect the answer is: "Not very well!"

So instead of criticism, try compliments! How about telling yourself, "I love you exactly as you are right now!" Again, I can hear you saying, "But I can't accept myself like THIS! I have a terrible complexion. I need to lose weight. I want to quit smoking. I can't love myself until I'm perfect!"

Aha! But here is the secret. You believe that you can't love yourself until you are perfect, but in reality, you can't wait until you're perfect to love yourself! Did you grasp that? Let's read that sentence again: You believe that you can't love yourself until you are perfect, but in reality, you can't wait until you are perfect to love yourself!

You absolutely can love yourself right now, exactly as you are, because you already are perfect! By loving yourself exactly as you are now, you might be surprised to find that you don't have the need to smoke, overeat, over-work, etc. You might just find yourself being the person you always wanted to be because you were really that person all along!

{
Follow your heart, *let your love lead* through the darkness, back to a place you once knew. I believe, I believe, *I believe in you.*
~ Excerpt of "I Believe in You" from the Lion King
}

Your idea of striving for "perfection" is the result of not feeling "good enough." I cannot emphasize ENOUGH that we are ENOUGH! [Pun intended!] We are ENOUGH, just as we are. We are PERFECT, just as we are! WE ARE PERFECTLY ENOUGH!!

So, let's work together to change those feelings of not being enough. It all starts with acceptance, approval and love of self. Whether it's the big mirror or the little mirror, whether it's silently

or out loud, whether you start out saying "love," or you substitute the words "accept and approve," JUST START! Come on, you can do it!

Since daily mirror work is essential, let's try making the process easier! If you are having trouble looking at yourself in the mirror to do this work, maybe one of these suggestions will help.

Try a baby step by using a small hand-held mirror or compact. It could be that for you that will not be as daunting as the big wall mirror in the bathroom or bedroom.

Another suggestion you might try is to make a large paper heart, cutting out part of the center of the heart. Then position and tape the heart on the mirror so that when you are standing and looking in the mirror, your face will be in the center of the heart. Write the words you want to say on a card strategically taped so that you can read them silently to yourself instead of saying them out loud.
You could try drawing the heart on the mirror with one of the easy-off markers so that your face would be in the center and then write the words with the marker off to the side or underneath the heart. When doing this method, you still have to frequently look back into your own eyes while saying the words.

Or, you might also just try saying the words silently to yourself looking right into either the small hand-held mirror or the large wall mirror. Start out silently, looking right into your eyes, as you tell yourself, "I love you exactly the way you are!"

And, if you just absolutely cannot bring yourself to use the word "love," try saying (for now), "I accept and approve of myself just the way I am." Then we can work up to love in a couple months!

When I was struggling to say those words to myself, I would remember how I always told my son how much I loved him, that I was proud of him, that I would always be there for him. So I would imagine that I was holding my baby self, or my little girl self, and

telling her the things that I had always so easily told my son. I would make my facial expression looking at myself in the mirror the same as when I had been holding him. I was shocked when I realized I had never said these words to myself or looked at myself with that type of loving expression.

I hope one of the above suggestions will assist you in beginning mirror work. The improvement in how you feel about yourself is indescribable!

 Self-approval and self-acceptance in the "now" are the keys to positive changes. You are ENOUGH! Whatever your current reality, YOU ARE ENOUGH! The past is finished. It's over and done and has no power over you. The POINT OF POWER FOR CHANGE IS NOW! Mirror work and affirmations are two of the methods to take your power back!

Forgiveness

As we are releasing the past, taking back our power and becoming our authentic self, another key step is forgiveness. Not only forgiveness of those we feel have harmed us or disempowered us, but also forgiveness of ourselves. Sometimes forgiveness of ourselves is the hardest step of all.

> {
> Forgiveness means
> *letting go* of the past.
> ~ Gerald Jampolsky
> }

Most of my life I've spent hiding... either figuratively or literally. I can remember when I was a child hiding in the closet or hiding under the bed. Then I "hid" behind layers of excess weight. For several years I hid from others by isolating myself in my house.

I hid my true beliefs because I just didn't fit in with my family or my community. I developed a false self that was "acceptable" to those

around me. I call that my "Eleanor Rigby" face. You know, the one I kept in a jar by the door?[16] I knew that if I let the "real me" show, I would be unacceptable and rejected. I accepted the beliefs of others as truth and believed that I was "not good enough."

As I was going through different phases and ways of punishing myself for not being good enough (which ranged from over-eating, over-working, inappropriate acting out sexually, abusive love relationships, spending money I didn't have, lots of surgical procedures and health issues, depression, depriving myself of pleasurable activities, etc.), the thought of forgiveness of myself and others was the furthest thought from my mind.

As I would discover on my personal healing journey, forgiveness was perhaps the hardest step of all. I learned that for me, forgiveness was a process done with baby steps until I was strong enough to fully embrace the feelings, the pain and the fear then let it go. A big stumbling block for me was the mistaken belief that forgiveness was letting others off the hook, that forgiveness would mean that what others had done to me was okay. It was "forgiving" what they did. The words, "I forgive you," were hollow and meaningless to me. I forgive you. Okay, so what? What happens now? The fairy-tale moment with a magic wand trailing stars and rainbows never occurred. Clearly, something was missing!

I tried "moving on," just forgetting about the things that were causing me pain. What I discovered was that by pushing the feelings away, they actually went deep inside me and festered, causing one physical symptom and problem after another. I tried to numb them out. I tried to push them down with food. I tried to distract myself with work and exercise. But I knew those techniques weren't working because my life wasn't getting better. My health wasn't getting better. If anything, my life and health were getting worse!

I did lots of reading and research about this elusive "forgiveness." I tried affirmations but they didn't seem to work for me. I tried beating pillows with my fists or hitting a chair with a plastic baseball bat; I just felt awkward and silly. I went to therapy but still had bouts of depression so severe that I would sit in a chair in my pajamas for days just staring into space, not bathing or changing clothes, barely eating. I went to retreats but always felt I didn't fit in. I tried meditation but found it difficult to quiet the running commentary in my mind.

There was still lots of anger and emotion about the wrongs I felt had been done to me, my feelings of not being good enough, and my feelings of not being lovable because I was "damaged goods" or "defective" in some way.

With each new method, I would be optimistic and think that THIS was the answer, but my life wasn't changing and I still had health challenges. In the final years before forgiveness of myself and others, in an act of desperation, I isolated myself by becoming reclusive, not allowing anyone in my life and not becoming a part of anyone else's life. To make sure I could keep people away, I allowed my body size to become morbidly obese.

For me, one of my first "Aha!" moments was the day I was sitting in my recliner, where I had been sitting and sleeping continuously for the previous five days, not showering or changing clothes, just sitting zoned out, staring off into space. I had been divorced for the second time, laid off from my job and feeling like an absolute failure of a human being. My son, who was a teenager at the time, came up to me and said, "Mom, we don't have anything to eat here except junk. Can't we get something healthy ... like some lettuce?" Wow. Out of the mouths of babes. That was a real jolt. Was it really that bad? Not only was I hurting myself, now I was hurting him as well.

As Wynona Judd sings in one of her songs, when you hit rock bottom, there's only two ways to go: straight up or sideways. Admittedly, I continued sideways for a long while after that day, but I was always searching for the answer. Little did I know that the answer was inside me all along.

Just like Dorothy in the Wizard of Oz searched for the way back to Kansas, only to find she had the answer all along, I searched for the way back to me, only to find "I" had been right there all along.

Remember what I stated previously? Everything we'll ever need is already inside of us, and everything we'll ever need to know, we already know. Dorothy and I both had the answer, we just didn't realize it!

The answer I found inside myself was facing the truth. Facing up to my authentic self. Feeling the feelings I had buried and hidden even from myself. I couldn't blame what I perceived as my failures in my life on everyone who had hurt me and disempowered me; I had a part in it as well. I had to take responsibility for MY PART in my life and then forgive myself along with others.

As I said, forgiving myself wasn't easy and it wasn't quick. But slowly I realized that everything that had happened to me, EVERYTHING, was an experience in learning about myself and in helping me develop lots of skills.

I had to forgive myself for being helpless and not being able to protect myself as a little girl. I had to forgive myself for inappropriate behavior when I was really seeking love and comfort. I had to forgive myself for unwise and hasty decisions in choosing partners.

I had to forgive myself for not being physically and/or emotionally available for my son during times when I now know that he really needed me. I had to forgive myself for hurting myself in all sorts of ways both physically and in my choice of life situations. I had to forgive myself for hiding – beginning as a little girl hiding under the bed and in the closet to an adult hiding in her house in a body with layers of fat as protection to keep others away.

And finally, I had to forgive myself for not knowing how to heal myself despite being intelligent, well-read, articulate, and in trying to heal others when I was the one needing healing.

> There is so much love in your heart
> that you could *heal the entire planet*.
> But for now, let us use this love to heal YOU.
>
> ~ Louise Hay

It wasn't until I was WILLING to love myself and truly willing to forgive myself for all my foibles, shortcomings and "sins," that I was then able to also forgive others and move forward on the path to healing.

I was led along this path, and when I was "ready," it seemed that a teacher or mentor (in the form of a person, a new book, or workshop) appeared to provide me a different piece of the puzzle where before nothing had worked. It is said that when the student is ready, the teacher will appear. I've had many teachers over the years, all of whom I am forever grateful to for the gifts and wisdom they have shared with me. I am sure that I will continue to have teachers and mentors helping me grow and move along my path.

I have confidence that when each of you are ready, you, too, will be led along the path, and at just the right moment, a teacher will appear to show you a different piece of the puzzle and help you with the next step. If you are experiencing a crisis or are just wanting to change your life, a good therapist or perhaps a Louise Hay Heal Your Life® Coach or workshop[17] may be of assistance to you. Hopefully at least one of the stories or ideas in this book, from all these wonderful women and teachers, will resonate with you and help you to take that next step on the path of loving and forgiving yourself.

Forgiveness is a gift you give to yourself. Forgiveness is being in the present moment. If we allow the thoughts of what others have done to us in the past to continue to punish us, we are living in a world that is over and done! The person we feel has wronged us probably isn't even thinking about it any longer. The person who criticized and belittled or judged us doesn't need to continue those judgments or criticisms any longer, because we are continually repeating their words in our head for them!

> *Practice enjoying the present moment,* rather than using it up consumed with guilt over the past or worry about the future. Refuse to allow any thoughts based on your past to define you.
>
> ~ Dr. Wayne Dyer

By persisting to think about past hurts and perceived wrongs either consciously or subconsciously, we are now inflicting the hurt on ourselves and accepting the opinions and actions of others as our truth. We repeat the story over and over and over so often, we accept it as our belief, and we live our lives as if it were true. That is when it becomes our false truth and our reality.

But what if we could rewrite the story? I'm not suggesting that we pretend things didn't happen, or that we change history. But what if we could change the RESULT of that history? What if we could change this false truth about ourselves that we've accepted as true based on the actions or beliefs of others?

I'm here to tell you from my own personal experience, it is absolutely possible! We do this by rewriting the false truth with a new truth. This is accomplished by learning to love yourself; by knowing that you are lovable and worthy because of and in spite of the things that have occurred in your past. Why? Because you are ENOUGH. You are perfect just the way you are. And, when you can fully embrace this, you can forgive not only yourself, but you can forgive others as well.

When you can accept that you had a part in the creation of all that you have experienced, then you can accept that you have a part in all that happens to you from this point forward. Our thoughts create our future. If our life and our experiences right now are the result of our thoughts the last second, the last minute, the last hour, the last day, the last month, the last year and so on, then it follows that our life and our experiences in the future will be the result of our thoughts in the next second, the next minute, the next hour, the next day, the next month, the next year and so on.

What do you want your life to be? Do you want it to be a life filled with bitterness, regret, sorrow, anxiety, fear and loneliness, or a life filled with satisfaction, happiness, peacefulness and love? The choice really is yours, and the point of power is NOW! I encourage you to live your authentic life, not the false life based on your perceptions and your acceptance of others' truths as your own.

> {
> You are in integrity when the life you live
> is an *authentic expression* of who you are.
> ~ Alan Cohen
> }

By learning to love yourself through awareness, mirror work and affirmations you can move to forgiving yourself and others, and be able to create the life you deserve to live! This doesn't mean that you won't have challenges or a life that is a bed of roses. After all, we are in this body and on this planet to experience and to learn, and there is no learning without challenges. Joseph Campbell said that where we stumble, therein lies our treasure.

It is how we PERCEIVE our challenges, and how we move through them, that is the determining factor of our enjoyment and love of life! Do you view your challenges as a burden or a gift? As you begin to view them as a gift, you will discover the treasure they contain.

Nurture Your Spiritual Nature

Remember that this is the mind-body-SPIRIT connection to wellness? We can't forget about our Spirit. We all have one you know! Teilhard de Chardin, the French priest, philosopher and mystic, said that we are not human beings having a spiritual experience, but spiritual beings having a human experience.

This means that our Spirit is here on earth to have a human experience, to encounter and go through as many of the human experiences as possible to advance on our spiritual path. Our Spirit didn't come to have an easy time, to never have challenges or trials and tribulations. Our Spirit came to learn as much as it could to advance on its spiritual path. (Boy, did I take that to heart! I think I got an A+ in going through as many experiences as possible!)

We need to nurture our Spirit as well as our bodies. We need to take time to smell the roses! We need to do whatever it is that will nurture our Spirit. For some, it might be walks in nature. For others, it might be yoga or meditation. For many, it is participating in organized religious and spiritual activities. Whatever it is that YOUR Spirit craves, by all means, indulge! Take care of your Spirit, and your Spirit will take care of you!

Many of you know Brett Michaels, the rocker (former lead singer of the rock group, Poison), who recently underwent several life-threatening events. Not long after, he was asked what advice he would give to others. This is what he said: "Enjoy the time you have left. Do what rocks your world!" I think that was "Rocker Wisdom" encouraging you to nurture your Spirit!

Four Steps to Creating the Life You Desire

In summary, I have identified and described four main steps to create the life you desire. The first step is recognizing your subconscious beliefs and thought patterns through learning the language of your body, listening to your body talk.

The second step is changing the beliefs and thought patterns that are leading to undesirable experiences and challenges in our lives through affirmations and mirror work.

The third step is forgiveness of yourself and others through understanding and accepting that you had a part in creating your history, and that you can rewrite your story to eliminate the false truths and beliefs of others.

The fourth step is nurturing and learning about your spiritual nature through yoga, meditation, participating in organized religious or spiritual activities, walks through nature, conferences and workshops with like-minded individuals – whatever feels nurturing to you.

A Wish, a Hope and a Prayer

In conclusion, my wish is that after reading all the sections of this book, you will be able to give yourself the gifts of healing, loving yourself and peace within. My hope is that with the power of forgiveness and re-writing your story, you will be able to live your authentic life. My prayer is that through healing, you will all be able to create the life of your dreams and do what rocks your world!

Rock on, my friends! Peace and blessings to each and every one of you. Namasté.

[1] ©January, 2011 Nancy Newman, Mindful Wellness, LLC

[2] *The Secret* is a 2006 book written by Rhonda Byrne, which reached the top of the *New York Times* bestseller list after being featured on the *Oprah* television show. A film by the same name was also released.

[3] Source: The Chopra Center, www.chopra.com

[4] *Magical Mind, Magical Body* by Dr. Deepak Chopra

[5] *The Biology of Belief* by Bruce H. Lipton, Ph.D.

[6] Gregg Braden, www.greggbraden.com

[7] *Language of the Divine Matrix* and *Divine Matrix: Bridging Time, Space, Miracles, and Belief*, by Gregg Braden.

[8] From the Centers for Disease Control website: Diethylstilbestrol (DES) is a synthetic estrogen that was developed to supplement a woman's natural estrogen production. First prescribed by physicians in 1938 for women who experienced miscarriages or premature deliveries, more than 30 years of research have confirmed that health risks are associated with DES exposure, including adult women exposed to DES in the womb being at an increased risk for cancer of the vagina and cervix.

[9] For more information, or to purchase *To A Child Love is Spelled T-I-M-E*, visit www.simpletruths.com

[10] As described by William Rand of The International Center for Reiki training, Reiki is a Japanese technique for stress reduction and relaxation that also promotes healing. The word Reiki is made of two Japanese words - Rei which means "God's Wisdom or the Higher Power" and Ki which is "life force energy." So Reiki is actually "spiritually guided life force energy."

[11] For more information on Toe Reading, go to www.toereadingonline.com . For information on becoming a Toe Reader, call the Southwest Institute for Healing Arts or visit the website at: www.swiha.edu.

[12] Source: *Heal Your Body*, by Louise L. Hay

[13] For more information about Cancer Treatment Centers of America, visit www.cancercenter.com

[14] All quotes from *Ordering From the Cosmic Kitchen* by Dr. Patricia Crane used with permission.

[15] To order any of Louise Hay's books on affirmations, visit www.hayhouse.com. To order Dr. Patricia Crane's book, visit www.orderingfromthecosmickitchen.com.

[16] From the song, "Eleanor Rigby," by the Beatles.

[17] To find a Heal Your Life® Coach or a Heal Your Life® workshop, go to www.healyourlifeworkshops.com.

Lisa A. Hardwick

Dedicated to all of those
who are suffering – may my
words bring you hope and light.

Chapter Two
I Don't Live Life – I Love Life

Chapter 2

I Don't Live Life –
I Love Life

{
Life is meaningless only

if we allow it to be. Each of us has

the power to give life meaning,

to make our time and our bodies and our

words into instruments of love and hope.

-Tom Head
}

What makes you alive?

Before I talk about my love for life and why I love it, I'd like to ask you: "What according to you is life?" Is life all about the scientific dictates of movement, growth, reproduction and eventual death? Are you a living entity simply because you can breathe? I wonder what your definition of life is.

I know one thing though and that is, science cannot define life in the sense that we know it. It cannot explain the trials and travails that every man and woman has to go through between the scientific milestones of birth and death.

Science may talk of growth in terms of cell division and body mass increase. It does not talk of growth in terms of pain and hurt, joy and happiness, dreams and ambition and other things that matter. It does not talk about spiritual and emotional growth.

Science may talk of the structure of the brain and the way information is transmitted and all things scientific. But, can science explain the thoughts that define every unique individual? Can it explain emotions? Can it tell you how your current circumstances will affect the person you are? There are still a lot of things science can't explain even today. How then, can we depend on science to tell us what our life means?

I personally feel that every life is unique. Everyone's definition of life also is unique. One way to look at it is like this: I do things my way. I get up in the morning at a certain time. I have a certain schedule to do things. I've had a childhood so very different from yours. It's obvious that every person's life has been very different from another's. How then can we all have the same definition for life?

I want you to now think back over the events in your life. Events that were good and bad, happy and sad, painful and exhilarating. Do it now. Once you've relived them, try to define your life. But wait. If you think your life has been exceedingly painful, do not relive only the sad and painful moments. I am sure there was at least one happy moment in your life, at least one good thing that happened to you. Think hard. On the other hand, if you think your life has been all peaches and cream, think hard for some painful memory (I am sure we all have them aplenty). Now, define life.

Why do I love life?

I love life. Before I tell you why I love life and what my definition of life is, I want to tell you a bit about my past.

My past is riddled with pain, unbearable pain that I trudged around with me for more time than I can remember. I remember the child I was, the pain I had. I remember weeping and weeping, knowing there was no one to help me. I was small, so small. It's that childhood I used to mourn for. I remember fighting the pain, but there's only so much a child can do. I used to sleep fitfully and get up in the morning filled with dread. One such morning, I couldn't take it anymore. I knelt and I knew that I was broken – broken beyond repair.

Twenty years ago, if I had told myself that I'd love that painful and broken part of my life, it would have reinforced my own perception of my "craziness." But, today, believe me when I say this: I love the pain that was such an integral part of my childhood. I am what I am today, because of that pain. It taught me survival. It taught me how to heal. It taught me how to hope and love. It made me Me.

For me life is love itself. Life is about hoping and dreaming. Hopes, · dreams and the promise of a brighter tomorrow is what makes me keep loving life. When I think of all that I had to go through in the past and compare it with what I have today, I can't help but love my life now.

I have people I love around me. I can share my love for life, calmness, hope and joy with others. I can look back at the painful phase of my life and not feel the heart-ache. I am a survivor, why would I not love life?

Earlier, when I used to look back at those years of my life and see the girl I was – broken, anxious and so much in need of love – I would weep till the sobs wracked my body and soul. But, I healed. The healing took time, and it was painful, so painful. I wanted to love the loveless child I was. And that is exactly what I did. I grew to love that child…I made my inner child – the hurt, battered one – love me. I made peace with my inner child…I made peace with myself.

There is one very important aspect to my love for life, and that is forgiveness. You can't heal until you forgive. You can't love until you forgive. Forgiveness is not forgetting. It's impossible to forget pain. If you've been through emotional and physical pain that makes you want to heal, you'll know what I am talking about. Yes, you can't forget pain, but you can forgive the one who gave you pain. And, when you start forgiving, the healing begins – the loving begins.

There is so much to love about life. Knowing my sons love me, knowing my friends care, knowing the beauty of a sunrise, knowing the calmness of a quiet night, knowing the feel of light breezes, knowing the awesomeness of a storm, knowing that so many people are happier because of the healing I could give them – how could I not love life?

Why do people hate life?

Most people I have come across want to be healed from their pain. They want happiness, joy, prosperity and all things good. But, they aren't ready to let go of the pain, they don't want to forgive. I can understand, believe me, I can. But, having been through it all, I know how important it is to forgive, to let go of the pain.

In my interactions with people, I have met very few who genuinely love life. Some of the reasons I found people hated life are the very ones that made me hate my life for more years than I can count. Do you hate your life because:

- You are in pain (emotional or physical)?
- YOU think you are not good enough?
- You think it is full of frustrations?
- You never get to do all that you want to do – there isn't enough time?
- You can't live with hurt – past and present?
- You don't have enough of something in life, be it money, luck, happiness, or anything else that your heart desires?
- Your life sucks, your relationships suck, your days are tiring and your nights restless and you simply can't take it anymore?

You could have one of the above reasons for not loving life or you could have some other reason for your hatred. I am not against hatred. If you hate something, you will work towards righting it. If you hate the way your life is right now, you will try to work towards making it better.

I fear for people who are indifferent and resigned, who cannot envision loving life, nor do they have the will power or strength to hate it. These are the people most in need of hope. Those who hate life need hope too, but I personally believe indifference and resignation are worse than hatred.

Are you resigned? Do you feel it does not matter if the pain that wracks your body stays on forever? Do you feel it does not matter if the hurts to your emotions do not cease? Do you feel you can go on with the kind of defeated persona you now have? Are you OK being the broken person you feel you are who can enjoy nothing in life?

I was resigned, too – I didn't mind residing my broken heart within my broken shell - Till the "voice" came my way. I had people who loved me, who stood by me through the darkness and yet I couldn't make myself become the Lisa I am today. The voice was my saving grace, it guided me to rise out of my stupor, it taught me to hope and love.

Even if you hate life and don't have a voice to guide you, you can still heal. Healing without a guiding force may be difficult, but it isn't impossible. If you fall within the resigned category, you wouldn't be holding this book. There is something about survival that attracts you. You know I've survived and healed, and you want to heal too. When you start to heal, you start to love. Together, we can all heal each other. Together we can love this world.

Do not go through life hating it. Identify where your hatred for life stems from. Once you know what the reason for your hatred for life is, start working towards eliminating it, improving it or replacing it as the case may be. Go on, a beautiful, hopeful and love-filled future awaits.

How can you start loving life?

Your son's teacher has summoned you for a one-to-one talk, you have a very important meeting scheduled in the afternoon, your tooth's been aching for days and you are stuck in traffic for what

seems like hours. Frustration, overwhelming frustration gnaws at you, screaming to be let out. How common is this scenario in your life?

I very strongly believe that life is beautiful. Every second, every moment that we breathe is filled with hope. Today might have been the most frustrating day of my life, but if I know that tomorrow might bring with it a beautiful sunrise that is worth staying alive to watch, life's beautiful.

Frustrations plague our lives day in and day out. I've lived through it. Now, I don't live frustrations, stress, sadness or pain, I live life. I sit back every so often and think of all that I am thankful for, and I surprise myself. I am thankful for many good things, but I am also thankful for the pain and sorrow that clouds my past.

But for the heart-wrenching pain and sorrow that marred my childhood, I wouldn't have been here. I wouldn't be filled with this hopelessly hopeful vision for life. I wouldn't have the loving heart that looks for ways to spread that love to others.

You may think I speak lightly of it now, but there was pain, there was suffering. I felt broken then, painfully broken. But I survived, and it's this survival that lends me strength today. It's my survival through the pains of my past that gives me renewed hope and makes me believe that I can not only survive through life, I can enjoy it. I have healed.

Think back to all the Thanksgiving dinners you have had in the past. How many times did your thanks include the fact that you were alive? Just alive and living? There was a time when I didn't want to live, when I got tired of putting up with pain day after day, when the mere thought of having to go through it for another moment was too much to bear.

But, I realize now that pain is transitory. You might be in the throes of pain, physical or emotional now. Remember, it will heal and you'll survive. One of the hindrances to a hopeful, brighter future is past pain.

If you've had pain in your past, let it go. Write all your pain down, read through it, relive it. Let heart-wracking sobs consume you; let them heal you. Then absolve yourself of all those destructive emotions by burning that paper. Watch as it burns and feel your pain burn with it.

Forgive all those who caused that pain. I know it's difficult, but that's what I did. Revenge is not sweet, love and forgiveness is. When you forgive, you give nothing to the person you've forgiven. You give something to yourself, you give yourself freedom – to dream, hope, live and love.

Life Takes You Somewhere

> In three words I can sum up *everything I've learned* about life: it goes on.
>
> - Robert Frost

Where are you headed?

I remember the time when I was so numb with pain that day and night made no difference. I lost track of myself and staying alive was simply a formality. In the midst of all that pain, when days for me were one continuous cycle of pain, hurt, anxiety and fear, life went on.

We've all heard it so many times that we consider it cliché: "Time and tide wait for no man." And yet, look at the wealth of meaning it has. When you are in pain or when you sit back thinking of your past pain and mulling over it every so often, you are losing out on precious time that you could use to right that pain.

Sometimes, pain is all that's left in your life. Sometimes, you are as helpless as I was, and don't know what to do. In those situations I pray that you get what you need most – love and hope. However, there are instances when we have a choice – to stay with the pain or let go. And it is surprising how many people continue to stay with pain. I stayed with my hurt, fears and pains for years, long after the cause had gone.

I could enumerate several reasons why you should let go of hurt, but here's just one that I want to share with you. Lugging past pain around stagnates you; your life cannot take you anywhere. Don't know what I am talking about?

Think of life as a tangible entity. For us, "we are and therefore life is." It should be, "life is and therefore we are." Life is not secondary. Imagine life as a pulsing power – a force that can do wonders. Life is not a state of being, it is a form of energy that can drive you in the direction you want to go.

But, look what happens to us when we stop wanting to go anywhere – we stagnate. The pain is so great, the hurt so strong, you shiver with fear or anger daily and eventually give up. This "giving up," this resignation, is what you should avoid. It's when you resign yourself to your fate that fate stops acting in your favor.

It's when resignation sets in, that life ceases to be the way we know it. We are all destined to know good in our lives, how much of it we actually see depends on when we give up when pain comes our way.

Now, analyze where you stand at the moment and where is life taking you. Has pain consumed you? Have you stagnated? Are you letting past pain stop life from taking you towards a better future? Or have you taken that healing step ahead and allowed life to take a turn for the good?

Love yourself, love the people in your life, love your life and your life will love you. When your life loves you, it will give you nothing but the best.

Why wanting only good things and good days in life is not a good idea

There are days and then there are days. Have you ever had a very good day – a day when you could forget all your pains and aches, both physical and emotional, and just enjoy what life had to bring? Did you want that day to last forever?

What's wrong with wanting happiness to last forever? Nothing, except that you'd stop feeling for others. Most of my love for others stems from my past, but every now and then something happens that makes me relive some part of that pain and it helps me understand the pain others are going through better. I then remember how important healing is and renew my efforts to spread it to others.

Besides, unless you share your happiness, joy, love and hope with others, it loses its appeal after a while. So, if pain comes your way, let it come. Tackle it. Don't let it overwhelm you.

Everything you do, everything you experience and everything you feel matters

Every event you've experienced, every thought you've thought, every acquaintance you've had has an impact on your future – no matter how small. Why are people told to keep company with good people? How does a childhood fear manifest itself in adult situations so often in medical cases? How does a certain smell, color or feature remind you of someone or something? That's because everything leaves an indelible effect on our lives.

You may not know why you cannot enjoy life the way you want to. Is there something that pulls you back each time? Some of the reasons why we can't do or enjoy something stems from something in our past.

One day when you are free from work and worries and can locate a quiet place in your house, do this small exercise:

1. Take a clean notebook and sit in a clutter-free room, which has a clutter-free table.

2. Place the book on the table, sit on a chair and do simple breathing exercises to calm yourself.

3. Next, start from your earliest memory, it could be from the time you were one year old or five years old, doesn't matter.

4. Write down the memories when you felt scared, fearful, angry, helpless, inferior, hurt, painful, unhappy, guilty or frustrated.

5. You might not remember all such instances, but note down all that you can.

6. Go through all the memories you've written. It's understandable that if there was a very hurtful memory in your past, you might feel sad and depending on the intensity of that hurt, it might reduce you to tears today. Let the tears come as you write and relive those memories.

7. Go through each of those memories and forgive all those who caused you that hurt, pain, unhappiness or fear. I know it is difficult, but sit there and say it aloud "I forgive you____." For instance, if your dad lost you in a mall (or if you thought he had at that time) when you were little, and you felt scared and thought your dad had left you and you remember it now, write it down. Say out loud, "I forgive you dad for losing me in the mall." Though this is a simple example, and you might not think it is important now, you never know the kind of impact it left on your subconscious. That you are remembering it now is proof of that impact.

8. Next, forgive yourself if the instance was a guilt-ridden one. If it was a situation where you were wronged, imagine yourself as that child and give that child your love. For instance, imagine the little you feeling lost in the mall. Go up to the little "you" and comfort her/him. Tell her you will love her and care for her. Tell her you'll take her home. Make little "you" happy.

9. Repeat this for every sad memory you have.

This exercise will help you consciously erase the unhappy subconscious memories that you carry around. These subconscious memories have the power to negatively impact our behavior, actions and thoughts today. Go on and do it. You'll make your life happier and life will take you somewhere – somewhere good.

Not everything works according to our plans - life has other plans for us

There were times when I wanted things to work my way. For the most part, I get what I want. All I needed to do is ask. Affirmation techniques have worked wonders for me and life hands me things I need out of the blue. However, there are times when I don't get what I want or things don't work out my way.

Do I get upset? Initially, I used to. But, with recognition of the fact that life has its own plans, I began to see the underlying currents by means of which life operates. If you don't get something you want, do not waste time and energy raving and ranting, or sitting and weeping.

More often than not, life has better plans for us. The worst situations can turn out to be the best if you'd only let life take its course once in a while.

When Past Hurts Overwhelm

> Have you ever been hurt
>
> and the place *tries to heal*
>
> a bit, and you just pull the
>
> scar off of it over and over again?
>
> -Rosa Parks

What happens when past pains and hurts come back? Look at the quote by Rosa Parks given above. How many of us identify with it? I do. For some unfathomable reason, we humans tend to keep unearthing past wounds and hurts as soon as they begin to heal. We like to wallow in self-pity. You may think I am harsh. I am not.

I can understand that you might be in the grips of the worst imaginable emotional or physical pain at the moment. That is a situation I've been through, and I have faith that you'll survive it, just as I have.

But, here I am talking of those who've left that pain behind, who no longer have any reason to be scared, hopeless or fearful and yet let their past pains and fears govern their life today. If there have been traumatic instances in your past, you cannot move past them if you continue to let those events dictate your thoughts today. I've been through it and I am grateful that I no longer have to go through the same. Today, the knowledge that I can survive is enough to give me strength to go on.

What happens to you when your past traumatic experiences, pains, hurts and fears come back to visit your subconscious? Do you:

- cry your heart out?
- cringe and avoid anyone and everyone?
- think you have it under control and walk around confidently while your heart is tearing up inside?
- become numb with pain and refuse to react?

Honestly speaking, if you cannot let your past pain go when it comes rushing back to you, I suggest you do the first option in the list above: Cry your heart out. Let yourself feel all that pain all over again. But before you break down, promise yourself that this is the last time you'll ever let that memory hurt you again. Then let it all out.

Cry a lifetime's worth for that memory. Go on and forgive whoever was responsible for giving you all that pain and love the "you" then. Imagine giving that younger "you" whatever is the cause of that memory. If there's fear, offer security. If there's emotional hurt, offer love. If there's neglect, offer your care.

Ways I used to counter past pain and hurts

I think I had more than my share of pains and hurts to contend with when I was a small child. I'd always felt that it was unfair that I should have to go through all that when I was far too young to understand what pain meant. Even after I'd left the pains and hurts behind, they continued to hound me. I lived because that was the least that was expected of me.

Those hurts don't bother me anymore because I've made peace with those hurts and with myself. Here's what I did to neutralize the pain and hurt from my past:

- I worked towards making myself more confident. One technique I swear by to increase your confidence levels is the mirror technique. Normally, most of us look at the mirror and see only the negative aspects of our body. None of us sees beyond the shell. In mirror talk, you stand in front of the mirror and tell yourself with conviction all that is good about you. If you have a pretty nose, say it out loud in front of the mirror. Basically, talk about everything that is good about you and feel nice about it – feel confident.

- I worked towards forgetting and forgiving my past, the way I've described earlier in this chapter.

- I worked towards reprogramming my subconscious. What do I mean by that? Our subconscious has been programmed in a certain way because of the pains and hurts of our past. There are ways by which you can undo that programming and reprogram your subconscious to your present scenario. For instance, perhaps you were locked in a room when you were small, and as a result of this incident, you now suffer from claustrophobia. You may feel that you are going to have this fear forever. That it is "just how I am, and I have to deal with it." This is where subconscious reprogramming comes in. It is possible to "reprogram" your subconscious to release this fear so that the instances that used to trigger the claustrophobic feelings, no longer have any effect on you.

- I learned to control my mind – not completely, but enough to be able to override its incessant negative chatter

- I learned to replace negative thoughts with positive ones. I recommend this one technique to most of those in need of healing. If you've suffered, you'll know how difficult it is to rid yourself of negative thoughts. Every time you realize you are thinking negative thoughts, replace them with positive ones. Initially, you'll have difficulty thinking up a positive thought, but as you go on, you'll get better at it.

Dreams Are Precious

{
Dream and give yourself
permission to envision
a You that you choose to be.

-Joy Page
}

What are dreams?

Do you dream? At night? Then, those aren't the dreams I am talking about. I am talking about the dreams you have during the day, dreams that you want to become reality. Some people dream of monetary gains, some dream of prosperity in every sense, some dream of freedom, some people dream of joy and happiness, some people dream of family well-being and so on and so forth.

Do you have dreams of that kind – dreams that you don't forget in the morning? Do you have dreams that follow you around? Do you have dreams that drive you day and night? If you do, then you have given your life a direction. It now depends on your life, where it wants to take you.

However, you cannot leave your dreams in the hands of life, fate or destiny, can you? I didn't. I am where I am, because I took charge. There are limitations. I can't be 100 percent in charge and I know it. Remember the part about life having its own plans for you?

Why should you dream?

Before I tell you how I took charge of my dreams and the course my life takes, I wonder why some people don't have dreams. Are you one of those who does not have a dream in life? I'd like to know why. Have you been through a lot of frustration, pain and hurt in life? Is that why you stopped expecting anything from life?

Whatever your reasons for the lack of dreams in your life may be, I'd really appreciate it, if you allowed yourself to dream. Dreaming and expecting something from life is a part of healing. It shows that you've reached a stage where you can see beyond the pain, beyond the hurt and see a future in which you'd want to be. Give yourself the permission to dream.

Dreams aren't a child's prerogative. You can dream too. There ARE castles, princes, and glass slippers in this world – you only need to ask.

How I follow my dreams

After I lived through the pain that marred my childhood and survived, I have a very positive attitude towards life. I have noticed that most of the times you only need to ask and you get it.
I practice what is popularly called positive affirmations. In positive affirmations, you make yourself believe that you are what you "want" to be. Here's what I mean. There was a time, when I didn't look the way I do today. I used the following positive affirmations: "I am beautiful. Every part of my body is perfect"…you get the drift?

Repeating positive affirmations allows your body, mind, soul and the Divine Energy work towards making it a reality. Positive affirmations need to be repeated regularly and without fail in a place that is quiet. You should be filled with conviction that the affirmation you are saying is true and will come true if it isn't already.

In the end, realizing your dreams boils down to the fact of how badly you want them to come true. Ask with all your asking power and believe in what you ask for and you'll get it. I wish you luck, as you embark upon your dream.

Pain is Sweet - Once Gone, It is Sweeter

> Many of us spend our whole lives running from feeling with the *mistaken belief* that you cannot bear the pain. But you have already borne the pain. What you have not done is feel all you are beyond the pain.
>
> - Saint Bartholomew

Why is pain sweet?

It seems really odd now that I should consider pain sweet. At one time, when I had to live through the pain, I couldn't trust myself to go through another day. Isn't it hypocritical of me? No, it isn't. There are things life teaches you as it walks you through the years and it has taught me the importance of the pain I had.

I do not mean to trivialize the trauma I faced or the hurt I had to go through, but when I think of the Lisa I've become because I went through that pain, I can see that life surely had a plan for me.

Pain is sweet because once you survive it, it makes you stronger. Once you survive, you are filled with unbeatable confidence and hope and those are qualities that don't come easily. Pain gets them for you. I agree, it is a hard journey to attain them, but once you've survived, hope can keep you up and running for years together – you need not fear any more pain.

Yes, pain is sweet and once it goes away, it is even sweeter. That's because, it leaves behind hope and where there's hope there'll be no more pain. So, if you find yourself in a painful situation at the moment, use positive affirmations to get out of it. Work hard and fight that pain. Survive. And when you survive, you'll know life is worth it.

What pain does to you – (it does not break you)

What does pain do to you? When I was at the receiving end of pain – a pain that made me hurt for years – I thought I would break. I couldn't take it anymore. But, I survived and it is this survival I share with people. I've made the pain a part of my past life.

I thought the pain had broken me – it hadn't. What do you think your pain does to you? Do not envision the worst. There's always hope, even in the worst situations and when faced with unanswerable questions there is hope. Hope remains.

Does your pain defeat you? Does it kill you from the inside? Does it numb you so much that you stop feeling anything but the pain? Hope and love can help you overcome pain.

Pain can be defeated, you'll be victorious. Pain can be killed, you'll be alive. Pain can be numbed, you'll feel. All you need to do is fight for survival. Sometimes, you can't fight and that is when hope becomes important. Hope that one day the pain will leave you and a happier future will be yours.

If the cause of your pain is in your past, then it's about time you worked towards overcoming it. Let the pain go. Yes, pain is sweet. But, once gone, it's sweeter.

How to live beyond pain?

If you want to live beyond pain, you could belong to one of these two categories:

- you had pain in your past and it continues to hound you
- you are suffering from pain now and can't enjoy life because it is so very intense

Depending on which category you belong to, living beyond pain would require a different approach.

If it's past pain that isn't letting you live life to the fullest, there's only one piece of advice I can give you: let it go. Let your past go, if it's so very painful. Don't learn to live beyond it, learn to live without it all together.

One of the most effective ways to let pain go is to forgive the person who caused you pain. It is also the most difficult. Most people stay with pain because it is comforting. No matter how improbable it sounds, it is true. Most of us are afraid of change, don't be. There is a very beautiful life beyond pain. Let that pain go. Live your life with your newfound freedom.

If pain is an integral part of your life at present then I would suggest you try to get out of it. In fact, I couldn't get rid of the pain that held me for years until I was lead by the inner guidance. But you can be strong even without an inner voice. Positive affirmations help a lot, use them in your quest for a solution to your painful problems. Keep hoping – hope will help you survive. Hope will also help you see beyond the problems that ravage your life.

As I Leave You Now...

May the love hidden deep inside your heart find the love waiting in your dreams. May the laughter that you find in your tomorrow wipe away the pain you find in your yesterdays.

That was all about me – my life, my pain, my thoughts. What about yours? Every life is unique, every person is unique and every pain

is unique. I don't know the intensity of your pain, nor do I know the cause. But, I do know that beyond pain is survival. I've survived, and I have helped many others survive.

There might be problems aplenty in your life, and I empathize with you. There is little I can do for you, but there is a lot you can do for yourself. You can hope and dream. You can love, you can live. Sometimes, living can become torture, something that you wish you didn't have to do.

Don't give up. When you cease living, pain wins. It can't and shouldn't. Fight your hurt, fight your fears. Rise to the challenge and give to yourself what you desire: freedom. Freedom from those demons from your past, freedom to hope, dream and love.

To be sure, there will be gut-wrenching moments - moments that will whisper in your ear: "All of that self-empowerment stuff is a joke... you are nothing; just face it that you are a failure and be done with it!" Thoughts and feelings like this, when they show up, can serve as an opportunity to utilize your God-given power to choose...to decide which thoughts and feelings you are going to endorse, or validate. Each and every time you recognize this, and then allow those thoughts and feelings that do not support you and the greater good of your life to simply exist, without feeling the need to fight with or resist them, you will find they fade as reliably as the light of the setting sun, each day.

It is only the thoughts and feelings that you give your "stamp of approval" and say "YES!" to, that have the power to influence or direct any aspect of your beautiful life.

The more you remember this, and activate your power of choice, the more you will find the light and warmth of peace, love, joy and happiness spreading through your heart...your chest...and like tender rootlets that are seeking life giving water, the very cells of your body will reach for, and connect with that light, and the feelings it carries on its luminescent waves of energy.

As you embark on your journey towards survival and a happier life, please know that I, Lisa Hardwick, send forth my love, and wish you beautiful healing.

Elaine Lemon

Dedicated to my beautiful children. I love you forever.

Bryce Lemon ~ Alyssa Lemon ~ Derek Lemon
Connor Lemon ~ McKell Lemon

{ Please always know that behind the ego struggling to survive, is *my soul longing* to mingle with yours. }
- Ram Dass

Chapter 3
Beauty is a Choice

Chapter 3

Beauty Is a Choice

Experiencing life as beautiful is a choice. We all travel this adventure called life in our own unique way; however, it begins and ends the same for everyone. We are born, we experience our journey, and at some point we all die. Though everyone lives a diversity of experiences affecting our self esteem and value, there is a way to create beauty out of pain, life out of loss, and love out of regret.

Learning to love not only our outer beauty, but also the beauty within, is the greatest way to fully embrace life. We have a divine birthright to live in an abundance of goodness, creativity, laughter, expression and love. How we respond to the deep pain from life situations is a proactive choice. The process of alchemy is what I desire to share; that is, shifting those experiences we have had that are viewed as demeaning or of little value and turning them into precious pearls of wisdom. The culmination of all the tragedies, pain, sadness and hurt we have witnessed in varying degrees, hold the very tools to experience our brightest triumphs.

I have explored my deepest, most painful moments throughout my life and found a way to forgive myself and others. I have lived the journey of an unstable childhood, leaving a marriage that did not work, being a single mother of five successful, intelligent children, buried my stillborn baby and healed several physical illnesses and life-threatening accidents. I am not just a cheerleader standing on the sidelines yelling motivational thoughts. I have walked through the fire and came out the other side knowing that the magnificence and power that life possesses comes from healing our negative patterns. I have chosen to reframe my paradigm by living a positive, thriving life.

Life is a discovery. When we decide to quit being a victim of our conditions by being accountable for our disappointments, we consciously choose a positive outcome. This opens the window for unseen forces to assist us to magnetize the beautiful life we desire. The adventure begins by uncovering core beliefs, mastering our negative thoughts, and having compassion and forgiveness for ourselves. It is one thing to dream but it takes courage to leap into the unknown and not settle for less than you desire. It teaches you to trust your inner knowing to navigate the way. There is a gift in all experiences. Expressing pure gratitude for our perceived suffering is the key to learn that life always says yes to me!

We all have a beautiful purpose longing to be expressed which brings joy and abundance to not only ourselves but also many others. May my words of love be a catalyst and inspiration to the discovery of your own inner essence that you are beyond beautiful.

Discovering Core Beliefs

{

Every great hero - past and present –
took a *difficult journey* of self awareness
before finding his or her rapture.

- Elizabeth Lesser

}

Everything in life has a vibration. We all attract experiences which resonate with our frequency. There is an abundant source of knowledge, wealth, health, and love available to everyone. Alignment with the frequency of our desires brings it into our space.

Our abundance is waiting to be given to us, always saying yes to our desires or our fears. The lives we live are the results of our beliefs about what we deserve.

We are in this life to learn specific traits in order to fulfill our purpose. We attract situations and lessons by holding a frequency that is in unison with what we believe we are worthy to receive. Not only are we affected from our early childhood experiences and conditioning, but also from unresolved emotional issues passed through our DNA. We can rewrite and heal both our experiences and DNA.

Bruce Lipton, Ph.D., stated in his book The Biology of Belief : "The genes and DNA do not control our biology; but instead, DNA is controlled by signals from outside the cell, including the energetic messages emanating from our positive and negative thoughts."

Once we have made a belief, we tune in to it, and only see those experiences which validate our truth. It is as if we have blinders on and even though other opportunities may be present, we are in harmony to our subconscious conviction of our conclusion.

{
Whether you believe you can

or you believe you can't,

you are right.

- Henry Ford
}

What we reflect and think about becomes our reality. Our current experiences are a result of our beliefs in the past. We can use this moment, the power of creation, to create our highest potential. All of our experiences hold the seedlings of opportunity. We must make a conscious choice to shift our ability to attract what we deserve. We do this by becoming aware of the negative patterns we have created in similar situations, and challenge the validity of our cynical beliefs.

Every experience we have stores information in our bodies through cellular memory. We can shift our cellular memory, call forth our deepest desire by learning from experiences, and turn our weaknesses into our greatest strengths. Because of the polarity we experience on earth, we have the advantage of feeling the depths of both extremes of emotion. The beauty is that our hardest, most difficult experiences also hold the potential for our tragedies to become our greatest growth.

We have within us the capacity to be whole, to experience healed lives of joy and abundance, and to live the purpose that our inner knowing has longed for. What if we choose these experiences to know the depth of them and then learn to radiate our truth as we intended? The problem is that most of us want to push this process away and avoid fully becoming who we are here to be.

As children, life is an adventure. A child has no inhibitions and eagerly desires to explore the new world around them. Imagine what beginning life would feel like, seeing and desiring to discover things that you have never seen before.

As I have traveled to several different countries in my lifetime, I have seen a small glimpse of how life is viewed as a child. Everything from plants, animals, behavior, and buildings were so foreign and new, I was intrigued. The more I observed, the more I desired to see the unique perspective of societies different from my own. I love new objects, attitudes, and cultures viewed for the first time. Being immersed within an unfamiliar way of existence, discovering why people do things and how they view life, my fascination about different parts of the world continued to grow. I am sure this feeling of adventure is similar to the feeling that children have.

A newborn baby trusts its caregiver to nurture, love and take care of its basic needs. As the baby begins to grow, it first attempts movements which stimulate its psychological, intellectual, and physical development. By a child doing a sequence of reflexes, it learns integration, growth, and maturity. Progression in movement in all stages of development is important for the learning to adapt to their external environment and evolve in their mental and physical

activity.

A baby begins by laying on his stomach and lifting his head, then lifting himself up on his arms, turning over, sitting, and then eventually desiring to get something he really wants, he instinctively makes movements toward scooting, crawling, standing, and walking, and in the process, becoming more capable of learning due to what it was he desired. Each part of development is based on mastering the previous steps of achievement and then pushing towards greater growth and expansion.

Even when a baby experiences the discouragement of falling down, his desire to explore continues and pushes him to attempt the movement again, thus integrating the process of growth and development.

A child doesn't say to himself, "I am so stupid; I screwed that up; I shouldn't even attempt it." As a baby develops, he continues to expand, watch, observe, and learn from past successes and take another risk to move to a different level. The key is that he continues those movements until it is mastered and becomes instinctual. He never focuses on the failures. The child does not have mental chatter or self talk about being inadequate, even when people laugh at him. The child simply laughs along with everyone, seeing the joy of the moment and the preciousness of the adventure. He repeats the movements until they become a natural flow of being.

Somewhere along our path, we began to internalize other people's reactions as negative thoughts and feelings about ourselves. Most of us have had trauma, abuse, or negative experiences in school, religious institutions, or family, and as a result, made conclusions that we were not okay the way we were. We hold those experiences as truth. We believe we are failures and what other people believe must be valid. We justify that we will never be good enough and slowly shut off the very nature that beckons us to move, explore, allow, and expand. Identifying the rules, structures, and even the painful experiences we have encountered allows us to challenge the limits we have made about our possibilities for growth.

We learned not to trust our inner knowing, our essential truth, and created a false identity, a persona, in an attempt to fit within the norms and expectations of others. Thus, we sacrifice an integral part of ourselves and lose touch with our divine essence.

There is a time and place for control because without boundaries and laws, there would be a lot of chaos in the world. However, much of our domestication has also created laws and limitations in our lives that sabotage our deepest desires of expression and creativity.

Watch a child and see their pure passion in the discovery of something new. Allow the inner child within you to emerge and have genuine expression, discovering what brings you the most joy. A child is free, living in the moment, not concerned about how it looks or what others think. Laugh with others when they laugh at you. When we observe all the ways we seek to protect ourselves from other's knowing our true authenticity, it is quite comical.

How would it feel to allow your true desire to be expressed through movement and exploration? How would being more childlike create freedom in your life? What limits have you put on yourself out of fear of other opinions?

Challenge Your Fears

{
Be not the slave of your past. Plunge into the *sublime seas*, dive deep and swim far, so you shall come back with self-respect, with *new power*, with an advanced experience that shall explain and overlook the old.

-Ralph Waldo Emerson
}

My son has had a poster on his wall for years of a snowboarder leaping off a snowy cliff. Every night as I tucked him in bed we would share time talking. I have always ended our conversation, quoting the poster: "Life is either a daring adventure or nothing." ~Helen Keller

I have taught my children to take risks from a young age. I have encouraged them to face their fears and know that there is nothing that says no to their desires except them. I have given them the best opportunities possible to defy the average thought and limitations of "I can't." My motto has been, "if you don't ask, you don't know," encouraging them to step into possibilities beyond the familiar.

Because of the limitations, rules, judgments and shame I felt as a child, my desire for my children to have a different upbringing has been fundamental. I have stood behind them adamantly telling them the world is theirs, and all they have to do is trust their desires.

At a time when I was going through my own personal rocky road, my son texted me that same message I used to quote to him: "Life is either a daring adventure or nothing." Not only was it payback time for a mom to know her child has listened, but also time to practice what I taught. It surprised me that the message I said almost every day came back to me, awakening in me the need to challenge the fear that was keeping me down. I was reminded of the value of remembering that in the strength of our own fears, there is a promise of an adventure awaiting. A death in a cycle is also the birth of something new.

Life presents itself with patterns based off of experiences and beliefs we have had for ourselves in the past. The cycles will continue to present themselves until we choose to heal them. As children, we make sense of our life by noticing and creating patterns. Many of these patterns are destructive and inhibit us from shifting the experiences we are having now to the experiences we desire.

Making a resolution to stop a pattern is not enough because when a similar situation occurs in our life which caused the dysfunctional pattern to first occur, we often respond in a similar way without a cognizant choice to heal the pattern. Becoming conscious of the pattern and then interrupting it by choosing a different behavior allows us to stop being a victim of our experiences.

How many times do we allow ourselves to listen to the ingrained messages and relive patterns of our parents, family or authority figures that have demeaned us, made us feel inferior, or told us we are not good enough? Do you allow expectations of others to influence the choices you make in your life? Trying to meet the expectations of others represses our own vitality and truth. Do you give up your power and dreams to be accepted by the ideals of others and fit within their paradigm of how you should be? Even though others may no longer be mistreating us, we play the same record over in our minds, giving ourselves excuses to be stuck and resist our own evolution.

Fear is really just energy that is trapped and not able to have movement. Think of fear as a fire. National Geographic did a study about animals in Africa that survived fires. The animals that run from the fire get exhausted and eventually collapse, unable to escape. However, the zebra is one of the animals that often makes it through the fire. The zebra turns, faces the fire and then runs through it. By doing this, it finds safety in the freshly charred earth that is ready for rebirth. Going through the fire shifts it from moving towards the animal to moving away from it. Running through the fire is the path to safety.

Our fears are usually irrational. They rarely are the life and death situations we conjure in our minds. By facing our fire, challenging it by moving through it, and learning the illusion behind it, we transform the energy. This awakens new possibilities for growth that were previously unavailable. The value of confronting our demons teaches us that we are always safe. Surrendering to our fear demonstrates to us that our resistance to the fear is what keeps it alive.

One way to deal with your fears is to ask yourself what is the worst thing that can happen in this situation? Take the journey in your mind on a downward spiral, imagining the most erroneous

condition that could occur. As you walk through the fire of the fear and observe how it feels deep inside, ask your fear what its message is for you. Be with the feeling of the fear, letting it pass through you without any judgment of yourself. Observing the feeling in the center of the fear allows the emotion to shift. Learning that even the worst-case scenario will not hurt your divine essence, teaches you to let go of the attachment.

There may be a trauma in that fear because something bad happened in the past. Terror shows up in your body attempting to protect it from happening again. However, confronting the energy transforms it. Observing your fear from deep within, holding a space of learning and love, educates you that in this moment everything is okay. Sending love to your angst is the key to releasing it. Being the victim of the fear is what keeps it connected.

After you have fully embraced your fear, take your fear on an upward spiral, releasing the binding effects on your behavior. Witnessing the worst-case scenario and discovering you will make it through that experience safely creates transition. The positive aspects of conquering your deepest fear are the source for beautiful opportunities to occur. Continue building the positive story until you see the gift that the fear has taught you. The complete opposite of the fear is one of your gifts. See yourself having the greatest experience possible by focusing on how much joy the transformation has brought you. The true gift is knowing your deep strength, your true nature and power to move through any pain or trauma.

What patterns seem to be consistent and repetitive, leaving you feeling enslaved to circumstances in your life?

What is the underlying fear which enables the recurring themes to continue in your life?

Compassion for Myself

> I learned that courage was
>
> not the absence of fear,
>
> but the triumph over it.
> The brave man is not who
>
> does not feel afraid,
>
> but he who conquers that fear.
>
> - Marianne Williamson

Deep within each of us is the belief that we are not good enough. Our challenge is to discover why we believe this message. Recognizing and healing these feelings teaches us we are the source for our approval and acceptance. The reason these feelings hurt so much is because we believe something that does not resonate with our true essence, the part that is completely whole and perfect.

My personal story of not being good enough was so ingrained in my mind, I remember thinking if I did not have these negative thoughts, there would be nothing to think. In my healing journey, when a negative thought crossed my mind, I would envision myself in the void, in complete darkness, peacefulness, experiencing no input coming in or out. Observing my breathing and becoming conscious of my body, allows me to recognize that in this moment I am safe and everything is perfect. This process has taught me how to let go of the mental chatter that has previously consumed me. Over time, I taught myself to be present through focusing on the fact that in this instant nothing is wrong.

Painful thoughts only exist in the past when we cling to thoughts of: "I should have, could have, would have," or if the future fear of "what if" exists. Fear never exists in the present. There are really only two emotions we have: feeling good or feeling bad. Deep in our hearts, we feel bad when we believe something about ourselves that is not true. Our deepest authentic self is always whole and perfect. Even if we have done something that is perceived as a mistake, it is really an opportunity to learn something more about ourself on a deeper level, to become introspective and decide whether the experience is working for you or not.

Perfection is not something to be achieved. Perfection is not about doing more or having more. Perfection is just being your true authentic self, exactly as you are now. The ideal time to begin is now because the present is the only time to influence a change in outcome. You cannot change the past, and you cannot control the future. But right now, in the present, you can make a conscious choice regarding how you feel and what you will focus on. Choosing a new behavior takes practice, and it begins with one step at a time.

I first chose to become conscious of whatever negative thought I was having, and just notice how many times that thought comes up. One time a day, I taught myself to notice my negative thought and purposely change to a new positive thought. We always have a choice about what we feel, but we cannot simply make a negative thought go away, we have to replace it with a positive thought and feeling to change our emotions.

Resistance

> Nonresistance is the key
> to the *greatest power*
> in the universe.
> -Eckhart Tolle

Defending our patterns and our resistance to challenging our limiting beliefs brings continuous disharmony in our well being. Healing can occur easily and simply when we are willing to look within. As we have the courage to acknowledge the wounded parts of ourselves, and replace those thoughts with positive experiences, it magnetizes success to be a continual part of our lives. Living in despair, depression, and anxiety feeds those feelings, because our thoughts and our attitudes create our emotions. The only way to really release ourselves from this cycle is to change our thoughts and experience happy situations that allow us to feel successful. Focusing our energy on positive, feel good experiences expands our capacity to experience more.

A Native American grandfather was talking to his grandson about how he felt about a tragedy. He said, 'I feel as if I have two wolves fighting in my heart. One wolf is the vengeful, angry, violent one. The other wolf is the loving, compassionate one.' The grandson asked him, 'Which wolf will win the fight in your heart?' The grandfather answered, 'The one I feed.' (Native American Proverb)

Like the wolves, we have two emotions fighting within us. We have a choice as to which emotion we will feed. We cannot feed both at the same time, it is not possible. If we focus on the bad feelings, then bad experiences grow, and we take a downward spiral toward all the things we are most scared of. When we focus on the positive experiences and opportunities that surround us, happy events increase. One positive experience builds another as we call forth synchronistic events that bring more joy and abundance in our lives.

When I was a teenager, one of my favorite things to do was to watch people. I enjoyed going to the mall and observing behaviors of others and eventually this evolved into a game with my friends. Being the tease that I can be, we decided to Super Glue a silver dollar right in the middle of the floor of the pathway in the mall. We sat on the benches engrossed with the humor of watching many come along.

Some kicked the silver dollar, some bent down and tried to inconspicuously pick it up, but they all scurried away in embarrassment. There were those that were absolutely determined they were going to get the silver dollar no matter what, bending down and digging at it as their frustration grew. They became so focused on the prize that they were completely oblivious to the commotion around them. Our scheme became a growing stratagem

of observing the desperation of people attempting to pick up the silver dollar off the floor.

One person after another furtively attempted to gather a small fortune. In my observations of our intentional pranks of provoking people, I discovered that some people aggressively go for what they want while others quickly back off due to other people mocking them. Though in hindsight, this wasn't the kindest thing to do, I learned a lot about people and the energy they hold about what they deserve in their life.

We have silver dollars on our paths all the time; our own limitations prevent us from creating a way to pick up them up. For most of us, the fear of others mocking us for attempting to get what we desire is what keeps us stuck. Even though it may feel like acquiring the silver dollar is impossible, there are avenues to getting our desires. Sometimes it just takes looking at it from a different perspective.

By practicing listening to your inner voice, you will know the way. Take a step forward, no matter how insignificant it may seem. It vibrates the frequency that we are willing to embrace our heart's desire. Seize the opportunities to claim your silver dollars in life. We are the only one who knows our inner longings, so despite what others think, claim the silver dollars of your heart's desire.

Does it ever feel like there is a silver dollar right in front of you and you can't pick it up?

How do you sabotage asking for and receiving the rewards you desire because of others' opinions about what you deserve?

How many times do you walk away from getting your silver dollar because it doesn't come easy?

Others' Opinions

> The world believes in finite resources and
> in everybody's guilt. As long as we adhere to
> these pernicious beliefs, we will not only fail to
> *let others shine,* but we will never be able to
> allow ourselves to shine fully either.
>
> - Marianne Williamson

People who have chosen to travel the safe side of the road in life often attempt to create obstacles for others who claim their desires. Those that mockingly observe our failure in living our dreams are toxic, and try to create embarrassment when we dream of our greatest treasure. These people are simply mirrors of ourselves and show us the doubts and fears we still have. We can use their resistance to strengthen our resolve to trust and follow our vision, or we can allow their mocking to stop us from achieving a goal. We always have a choice.

Be aware that other people's fear of our success really has to do with their own fear of either losing you if you succeed, or their own refusal to be accountable for their own attributes. As a result, they attempt to project their feelings of what they feel they deserve on us. Recognizing this, we can choose to not take what others say personally. They are simply telling a story about how they feel within. Sending increased love towards those who oppose our growth is the answer to being free. It gives us permission to let go of their doubts and fears and trust our inner knowing.

When we do allow the opinions of others to infiltrate our lives, doubts begin to grow bigger and bigger. We eventually question everything we have come to know about ourselves. Questioning our own strength and ability to stand in our own power hinders our progress of development.

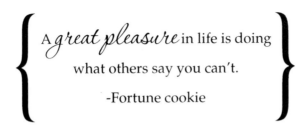

{ A *great pleasure* in life is doing
what others say you can't.

-Fortune cookie }

There was a time I let someone else's opinions deflate my world, which created a downward cycle of despair. I felt destroyed physically, emotionally, mentally, and spiritually. What we are experiencing in our outside world is simply a reflection of what we feel inside. Making a list of all the things my heart has yearned to express allowed me to realize I was giving my power to someone else.

A tool I have often used to heal myself is to sit in front of a mirror and look deeply in my eyes, adamantly claiming what I deserve. Forgiving ourselves for believing untruths that do not align with our beauty within creates healing. Other's projections of lack do not have to be ours. When we allow others' negative influence to resonate with our wounded inner child, it is very painful.

We have a choice to stand in our power and be awakened to our inner truth, or we can be destroyed by other's beliefs. Being accountable for the experiences we have had supports greater awareness in our life. Blaming others for what has occurred continues the cycle. We call forth certain people in our lives to challenge our deepest fears. Ignoring the red flags of our inner knowing and not listening to our intuition opens a space for difficult lessons to occur.

Forgiveness for others is not saying that the situation that happened is okay, it is simply declaring that I will not continue to give energy to the experience. Honoring and loving them for the lessons they have given us allows us to be free. Being responsible for our own choices is a liberating reality.

How many times do we allow ourselves to let people infiltrate our lives and take away the passion we were living? We have all been taught that being around people when they are ill can also make us sick. As we permit people with lower vibrations to infiltrate our lives, we eventually lower our own vibration. There is an equalization of energy.

Surrounding ourselves with people with like energy allows us to hold higher thoughts and vibrations. We are all radiating a frequency that when in tune, is in harmony with our deepest desires. Spending time with similar thoughts and frequencies creates a balance in our energy that either takes us higher or lower.

Compassion and forgiveness of ourselves for not seeing who we really are is a gift that teaches our inner light to shine. What beliefs are you defending? We do not need to be submissive to the power of others. Trusting our inner knowing is the truest source of love. Taking a stand for our individual strength and maintaining our true identity is where we find our power to create.

As our authentic self emerges, we claim our life to be lived in celebration of ourselves. Vibrationally and consciously we must all radiate our own truth. Listening to our intuition, we learn to embody the full essence of our being.

Practice thinking about floating in space, just being, with no input or output. How does it feel to just be present with your body? Bringing yourself to the moment of now allows all the mind chatter to cease. Notice that right now, in this moment, there is nothing wrong. In this moment you can be perfect and love yourself exactly as you are. You are a divine being with all the power within to experience life as you desire.

Finding The Gift

{
You can't get rid of negatives by forcing,

resisting, or denying; instead, find a way to turn

them into positives. Take the raw materials before

you and *transform them* into their highest potential.
}

- Alan Cohen

We are vibrating energy, subconsciously communicating messages through body language and actions, as well as words. Most people are not aware of the energies we are perceiving. If I am open to receiving, everyone I meet has a gift to offer me. The time I have to connect with them doesn't matter, they have something to teach me about myself. People are mirrors for us, and we see in them a part of who we are. We project feelings and thoughts on them that may or may not be true for them because of the way we feel about ourselves.

When we are open and receptive to love, it opens a space to bring in more love. It is the receptivity that allows the flow of energy to connect. Being in a place of love for ourselves and others creates a state of flow of abundance.

We all play an integral role in others' development. Choosing to show up in love, receptivity and giving creates a space of growth for everyone. This does not mean that you engage in their complaining behavior or accommodate when they are reacting in a way that distracts you from your purpose. It means looking for the beauty each soul carries, free of judgment. Seizing opportunities to serve always opens new experiences for our own growth.

When I felt everything in my life had reached an all-time low, I could barely even get out of bed and out from under the covers. It felt like everything that could possibly go wrong was – and fast! I was deep in the midst of a downward spiral of chaos and change. I didn't know how I was going to buy food for my children, I was extremely ill and unable to work and I was barely able to sit or stand because of the pain from a severe car accident. In the midst of the storm, it was hard to see beyond the reality of what was staring me in the face. Chaos in our lives always opens opportunities to give birth to something new.

In my quiet moments of meditation, I was seeking higher guidance. I was told there was someone else that felt worse than I did and to focus love there instead. I took the few dollars I had left and bought lilies at the store. This small token was a stretch of faith for me. I gathered three of my children and went to the assisted living center close by. My heart had guided me to someone there who was feeling the way I was feeling. My intent was to make her day special.

As we walked in, immediately I knew who we were there for. She sat in the corner by herself, walker close by, staring at the darkness outside the window. We approached her and gave her the flowers. She absolutely gleamed in amazement. She asked if that was us that drove in just a few minutes ago, and we told her it was. She then said that she had just been praying that the person in the car was there for her. She was delighted by the smell of her flowers and kept repeating over and over, "I can't believe it." Seeing the joy and pleasure she had experienced in our few minutes of sharing shifted my entire being from focusing on my despair to sharing love.

She did not know the gift she gave me that day. For the first time in months my broken heart had been healed and the deep hurt and despair that resonated from my soul had dissipated. I watched her as the light we ignited within her began to spread throughout the assisted living center. She introduced us to friends, who were also happy to see us. It was like throwing a pebble in a pond, the ripples reached out to many, lifting hearts and souls of so many more than the one person I had intended.

Greater yet, I came to my own self discovery; my previous desire to pull in and shut down because of my deep sadness and pain had ceased because I unconditionally loved another. I learned a huge lesson that day. A fragile lady in an assisted living center that I went to serve, had given a gift to me. She showed me the pure love and joy that came from caring enough to lift someone else's burden. In that moment of offering a small gesture of love, she gave me a gift to lift myself.

I wrote in my journal, " I smiled today for the first time in months. I can always serve and create beauty when I come from the depths of my love within. Love is all we have. Tomorrow, I will love again."

Living Your Dream

> Risk more than others think is safe.
>
> Dream more than others think is practical
>
> Care more than others think is wise.
>
> Desire more than others think is possible...
>
> and *the universe is yours.*
>
> - Author unknown

Identifying our dreams and desires is the first step to manifesting. You can usually find your greatest dreams in the areas in which you feel disappointment from the past. This is simply energy that has not had completion in its expression. Looking at what you were passionate about when you were younger is a good place to begin. Somewhere along the way you told yourself you could not do something, you did not deserve it, or were criticized for your behavior. Acknowledging your progression and giving yourself permission to embody your truth is the perfect place to start. In our failures are hidden treasures of our soul's longing for expression.

What have you always wanted to do that you told yourself could not be accomplished?

What area in your life did you use to have great passion for and then gave up on the dream?

Identifying where life has defeated you and then challenging it deeply is where your truest talents lie. Alchemy is defined as the process of transforming something perceived as little value into a substance of great value. We all have the power within us to make a metamorphosis of our lives. One of the greatest purposes of life is to boldly defy the limitations we have been bound to.

Question what it is that you have always wanted. The more specific you see your dreams and all the details of your truest desires, and knowing that you can have this dream or better; the more you are able to visualize and focus the energy that brings abundance to you. We are the creators of our experiences. There are forces in the universe which bring what we focus on into our reality. Your inner knowing has all the answers inside your heart. We must first ask the questions so that we are very clear about the intention of our dreams, visualize and feel what it feels like to be in that vibration. Knowing something is yours activates the very power that draws your dreams to you.

Controlling the Outcome

There is a delicate balance of allowing the Source to bring us what we desire versus controlling the outcome. Even though we have had a specific vision of our dreams, being attached to how it has to be manifested blocks the flow of abundance. When we are in a space of trusting our higher self, events synchronize.

The only thing that is constant in this world is change. We anticipate change, desire it, fantasize about it, but when it is right in front of our face, do we decide we can take advantage of the new opportunity or stay in our comfort zone? The comfort zone is not necessarily a comfortable place, but it is an experience that we are familiar with. As we try to stay in the same experiences where we can predict the outcome, it also limits our ability to creatively express and grow.

Every cycle in life is about birth, growth, evolution, death, and then rebirth. Yet, how many times do we resist the very thing that will bring us the most growth? We remember the past and desperately cling to being safe. Staying safe is painful. Staying safe keeps us small.

When I traveled to China, many of the old women had difficulties walking because of their practice of binding their feet throughout childhood and puberty so their feet would remain small. Small

feet are culturally beautiful in that country. Not too many years ago, women in the United States wore tight corsets to keep their waists small. The belief that we have to stop the natural state of our individual evolution is appalling, binding our expression of beauty to fit within the norms of society. Not only are we accepting the collective consciousness of "how we should be," but also claiming that our individuality is not okay.

Authenticity is the only way to fully live life. Nobody is content with an ordinary life. We are shown and taught through the media and other sources what ordinary looks like. It has been ingrained in most of us to live life in a certain way through the expectations and teachings of parents, schools, religious organizations, and other institutions in society. There is something within each of us that has a deeper longing for the true expression. Truth cannot be discovered. Truth is constant. Truth is revealed as we let go of the lies.

What have you always longed for?

If there were no limitations in your life, how would you truly be living?

What makes you passionate? What brings you the most joy? What was your passion as a child, your fantasy of what you would become?

What is the dream you never realized that still creates the longing inside of you?

> The *greatest gift* you give others is the example of your own life working.
> - Author Unknown

The Leap

The jump is so frightening between

where I am and where I long

to be. Because of *all I may become,*

I will close my eyes and leap!

-Mary Anne Radmacher

When I was 18, I decided I wanted to go sky diving. I was excited and talked about it continuously with my friends, anticipated what it would feel like, but eventually I allowed my fears to overtake me. I was afraid and chose not to go. The thoughts about sky diving didn't leave though. I began to grow fears in my mind about what would happen if the dive wasn't successful. I imagined standing at the door of the plane, the wind blowing on me and feeling an overwhelming fear to jump.

This fear grew and grew within in me until the point that even watching movies about sky divers jumping brought on a panic attack. However, my favorite part was watching them after the jump, reaching the point of free fall. Something within me loved viewing sky divers after the adrenaline rush as they peacefully floated down, blissfully observing the world from a different perspective, beholding how small life really is.

When my daughter was 18, she decided the gift she wanted for her birthday was to skydive with me! Petrified, I chose to take the challenge and booked us a week ahead. I was keeping it as a surprise for her but told others. Every time anyone brought up the subject, I had a panic attack again. The fear would overcome me, replaying all my past horrors of the various outcomes. Finally, the night before the big jump, I read in *A Call To Power* by Sharon McEreane these inspirational words:

> In learning to fiercely attack
> your *personal fear* of the unknown,
> the wings of your soul will be
> supported by the ever present breezes
> which are the breath of Great Spirit.
> -Sharon McEreane

Arriving at the sky diving school, we put on our jump suits and watched a video about what we were going to do, given a few instructions, and then climbed into the plane. That is all the preparation we were given. I was desperately trying to stay in the moment and breathe through the experience, but as we arrived at our 13,500 foot destination, the door was opened. Sitting right next to the open door for five minutes, feeling the intense wind, I could sense the height of the plunge before me, and my heart was pounding like never before.

I was strapped on to the man I was jumping tandem with. I went to the door challenging one of the greatest fears I had had for years. My anticipation of the jump was overwhelming, my body was shaking and stomach clenching. I began to think I couldn't do it. Then the instructor told me to lay my head back and rest it on his shoulder.

In that moment of my surrender, he jumped. I was pulled free from the safety of the aircraft and thrown into the unknown, plummeting in free fall. The wind raced past me. I couldn't catch my breath and for the 30 seconds of exhilaration during the descent, I felt like it would never end. Finally, he pulled the parachute out.

The peaceful feeling of floating was elating, seeing the world as I had always imagined. I noticed that being above all the chaos of life, everything was peaceful and blissful. I was above the fears and the drama of life, serenity engulfed me as we slowly drifted down. That day, I saw life from a different perspective. Problems that seemed so big were minuscule. The moment I was experiencing was the only thing that mattered. No fears of the past or worries of the future existed. I was living a dream I had anticipated for years. What I had previously perceived as being so frightening was exhilarating. I was dumbfounded to realize I had spent so much of my time avoiding one of the greatest moments in my life. As we approached the ground, things got bigger and bigger, and then we finally landed in the field where we were back to reality again.

How many times do we spend our life avoiding the very thing that will set us free? Many times we focus on our greatest fears so much that we attract them into our lives in order to conquer them. Just as I had been challenged by sitting next to the open door in the plane with the wind blowing in my face and my heart rapidly racing, opportunities present themselves in our lives so we can conquer our fears. The real question is whether we dare to take the leap. Have you ever considered that the obstacle which scares you the most is perhaps where your greatest gift lies?

We all want to know that there will be a parachute to catch us. By taking a leap into the unknown, trusting our inner knowing and the direction life is taking us, we acknowledge nothing can be taken away from us. You cannot lose your real treasure, which is your authenticity.

> He has not learned the *lesson of life* who does not every day surmount a fear.
> -Ralph Waldo Emerson

Avoiding the experiences we fear the most wastes the energy we could be spending on fulfilling our potential. Preventing rejection, fear of failure, people and situations that could hurt us makes us stay stuck in our lives. Releasing the core beliefs about ourselves opens possibilities for growth and achievement.

We all have a story about our life. It is just a story. It may feel real because for most of us, the pain is still present. The event happened

in the past. We have a choice to continue reliving this story over again, which eventually destroys us, or to challenge the judgment we have made about ourselves based on our story. Conclusions that we made at a very young age continue to be present as long as we give them energy or avoid them. When you heal the core beliefs you feel by bringing them to your awareness, the memories of the experiences are still there but the pain around the issue is no longer present. Even though a similar experience may occur, the recovery from the situation is faster.

Many times we perceive those experiences which challenge our fears as obstacles. What if we looked at it from a different perspective? Being above the earth in my parachute gave me a new outlook about how small everything we do in life is. When we are involved in the chaos and craziness in every day experiences, it makes it difficult to stop and observe it from an outside view.

Imagine for a moment that you can look at your difficulties from a different awareness, observing and noticing the conclusions you are making. An outside perspective, observing from a place of non-judgment, allows you to shift your paradigm so the situation is not so complicated. We are constantly attracting situations to challenge and liberate our view. Clearly seeing the limitations we have made about a situation and questioning the conclusion we have made about ourselves is the path to wholeness.

{
You gain strength, experience,

and confidence by every experience

where you really stop to *look fear in the face.*

You must do the thing you cannot do.

-Eleanor Roosevelt
}

Obstacles arise in our lives so we will take a deep introspection within and observe our defenses, habits, and convictions. This process allows us to release the patterns and align with our true purpose and desires. Looking deeply within and discovering what we perceive as darkness, mistakes, failures, or rejection is an opportunity to change our conclusions and be free.

What experiences have you perceived as obstacles in your life?

What have you learned is most important to you through facing your fears?

How has a situation that frightened you allowed you to gain strength?

What personal story forced you to deeply look at and challenge your fears?

Why Settle?

{
What is outrageous is not

what you ask for. What is

outrageous is what you settle for.

-Alan Cohen
}

We all have a choice to rewrite our script in life to a positive one. While everyone has experienced deep conflict and problems, some of us internalize those experiences and choose our identity as one of "victim." There are others who have chosen to learn from the experience and awaken to a deeper truth that lives within. Our wholeness is always present, remembering our perfection awakens our true expression of individuality and purpose. Being a free spirit gives us permission to follow our own knowing, despite what others think. Consciously choosing what is best for us brings more good to our lives.

I was visiting Los Angeles and checked out late from my hotel to head to the beach before my flight. I was starving, it was after noon, and I still hadn't had anything to eat. I was looking for places to eat

along the road when I saw a fast food restaurant. The thought of putting that kind of food in my healthy body was repulsive. I had worked so hard to get balanced and healthy. I kept driving.

Finally, I had reached the point of starvation. I wasn't sure if I was ever going to find healthy food. Right then, another fast food restaurant was in front me. The thought of eating the greasy food, the heaviness and bloating I would feel afterward and the disturbing feeling of fullness the food brings came to my mind. I knew that I could just get over my pain of "starving" by pulling in. In that moment, I made the decision to find something to eat; however, I was not willing to sacrifice what is best for me for the feeling of being satisfied for the moment. I kept driving.

To my surprise, five minutes down the road I found a health food super market. I couldn't believe it. I not only had a healthy choice, but an abundance of healthy choices. I bought some fresh food that was nourishing and tasted great. It was so divine. I spent the day at the beach enjoying the beautiful ocean that I love and also eating a meal that respected myself and my body.

On my way back to the airport, I saw the fast food restaurants again. I realized that I could have given up and settled for something that was easy and convenient, but this would have made me sick again, creating another cycle of needing to cleanse my body.

The paradox hit me: When I have a dream that I really desire to manifest and I am focused on that goal, if I settle for something else just because it is convenient and available, I am detoured from my dream. Staying focused on what I really want brings me a multitude of healthy choices. I vowed in that moment to honor myself and keep focused on my dreams.

There have been plenty of opportunities for me to eat from the greasy spoon in life. If I left an experience because I knew I could have more joy, how can I possibly settle for anything less than more joy? Every time I stop and eat at the places that do not nourish me, I am sending the resonance that I do not trust life to deliver what would make me most happy. This is similar to accepting something in my life that is only a part of my dream and trying to convince myself that I can live with it. Following through and focusing on my desired outcome, trusting that my truest desires will come to fruition, will bring to me what I really want.

If we continue to reflect on experiences we have had and people that hold us small, we will constantly miss the opportunities that are now present for us to embrace. We are always given opportunities to make changes, but when we focus on how we can't, fear from the past keeps us from embracing the now. In this moment we have the power to create whatever we focus on by visualizing it, feeling and enjoying our creation.

Our inner truth desires us to experience the most joy that we can hold. If I really ask for what I desire or something even better, I will always be challenged to see if I am serious. I will be given opportunities to choose a lower vibration again or hold the space for my true dream to manifest.

We all have special skills and abilities. People who succeed will embrace and enhance their abilities. Settling for something easy instead of focusing on their truest desire creates an average life. One of our biggest challenges is allowing our dreams to be expansive and not limiting them, despite opinions of what is practical. Holding the vision of what we want and creating the picture allows the universe to bring exactly what we are calling forth.

All the answers are within, and as we follow our inner wisdom, we can use our resources and inner strengths to bring us our heart's desire. The challenge is to make ourselves the authority instead of allowing someone else to be.

I have a client that has repeatedly told me that she can't accomplish her goals because "They" all say she can't. I always ask her, "Who are they?" Then I explain that "They" are the people who have chosen to live small. Permitting others to set limitations on our life based on our own fears is perhaps one of the greatest obstacles we face.

Imagine you are a butterfly, and you are trying to tell the caterpillar what it is like to fly. The caterpillar has no thought form or brain

frequency to resonate with flying because it has not experienced it. It does not mean that the butterfly is wrong or can't fly just because the caterpillar does not agree. The caterpillar simply does not see life from the same point of view. Why do we repeatedly allow those who have not experienced life from our perspective to influence what our heart is calling us to do? Our inner wisdom knows the way. Within our souls is the blueprint of the life we are born to live. We all have a contribution to bring to this world which brings a greater amount of joy and love to ourselves and others.

Fulfilling our life's purpose is our highest priority. Every experience in our life has laid the foundation for the unfolding of our path. Celebrating where we are right now, and trusting that all of our experiences are a culmination which created the evolution of ourselves now, is an important step. The more we value and honor our creativity, allow our unique contribution to the world to shine, and are in alignment with our desires, we create joy and abundance in the world.

What activities do you really love?

What step can you make now to express your inner strengths more fully?

What resources do you have right in front of you that you have not been willing to see because it seemed too easy?

Stop Trying

{
No problem can be solved from the same level

of *consciousness* that created it.

-Albert Einstein
}

I opened my door one day to discover a beautiful blue bird which followed me inside my house. I have always loved birds, so I enjoyed it for a while. My large vaulted ceilings gave it an ample amount of room to fly around. However, after a time, I noticed it was trying to escape through my clean windows to freedom. My attempts to shoo it to the open door were futile. I noticed the bird become exhausted as it continued to attempt to exit through glass panes. I opened windows and screens to see if I could encourage the bird to get free.

As the day continued, the bird became relentless for its natural desire to fly free. My annoyance and preoccupation with getting the bird out of my home also consumed my day. I really didn't have time to dedicate to saving a bird, although my love for the bird became my focus. Over and over it flew from window to window, hitting the glass and then quickly going to the next window.

I was concerned for the well being of the bird, not to mention the droppings that would be left behind throughout my home. Every opportunity I provided for it to escape, the bird's fear of the circumstance made it more panicked, as if I was threatening its life. Instead of the bird resting and taking its time to navigate to freedom, it flapped its wings wildly and continued its pattern faster and faster flying from one end of the house to another, hitting the window panes.

It was clear to me, that all it had to do was follow the path to where the wind lightly blew through the open doors and windows. After several hours I gave up and decided that the bird was my guest for a while and went about my day. Finally, the bird stopped its desperate panicked attempt to escape my home. The bird sat high on one of my ledges, breathing deeply and in a space of acceptance of its fate, it rested and observed. Suddenly, with no thought at all, the bird flew straight out of the front door and was free! Once outside it sat in a big tree next to my door, as if nothing had ever happened, and in a few moments it was gone.

I thought about the lesson the bird had taught me. This bird did not intend to enter my home, but once it had, it reverted to its primal survival mechanisms, needing to escape no matter what. I was not holding it captive, but in its fight-or-flight response, it perceived everything to be a danger. In that space, the bird did not tune into its natural knowing but instead went into survival mode. It continually

attempted to escape from my home over and over by hitting closed windows that obviously were not the answer to freedom. Continuing to attempt escape the same way clearly seemed to be its only answer. It wasn't until it was able to calm down that it recognized that its inner knowing knew exactly how to move out of my home and back to freedom.

How many times in our life do we find ourselves with a problem that we continually seek to resolve by approaching it in the same way? We do it so much that we do not even realize that there are other open doors and windows for us. There is not just one way to get through a situation. In a panic, we do not recognize people that love us and are willing to assist us to move through to a different space.

We become so sure within ourselves that the only way to conquer a problem is to figure it out alone. In that mind set, there are many failures we make, taking us to another dead-end that leaves us frustrated, hurt and worn out because we keep trying. Finally, we reach the point of exhaustion. If we could stop for a minute and go inward asking our deep inner knowing to show us a way, we wouldn't have to try so hard.

Does it ever feel like trying is what gets in the way? How many times have you desired to have a different result in your life but you keep trying to do it the same way you always have? Does the feeling of complete collapse overwhelm you to the point that you just sit on the edge of what you desire, even watch someone else easily accomplishing your heart's desire and feel frustrated that you can never get there? Do you have people who love and care for you that seek to guide you easily and simply through the threshold of freedom, but your attitude of knowing better keeps you in the same place where you first began?

Every time we try to make a major change in an area of our life and approach it the same way that we have done in the past, we will stay stuck exactly where we are.

Change occurs with ease by looking at a problem from a different state of awareness. Through self examination and discovery, we can break through many of our behaviors we desire to change. Our limitations occur at a time in our lives when burying the issue deeper inside felt like the easiest route. Buried feelings within do not go away. They are held safely in our cellular memory waiting for the perfect time to resurface so that we can heal and become conscious of the belief, and learn from the lesson we created.

How much do you desire this change? How is change important to you? Is this a true desire? Do you feel that ignoring the problem will magically make the problem disappear? Do you choose to live life safe because it is familiar? Making that change is a challenge because we have to move beyond the safety net that really keeps us stuck.

Do you have friends and associates that are already doing what you desire? Have you even considered that being in the energy of those individuals who have already accomplished your desires, aligns you closer to creating your accomplishment? Personal coaches and true friends are helpful to assist you to see things from a different point of view.

In the past, I feared those who had already accomplished the goals I wanted to accomplish. I thought these people were scary, and I felt intimidated by them. Then my inner knowing reminded me to celebrate the fact that people in my space are enjoying the things that I desire. Honoring others' accomplishments and supporting them aligns us to a similar frequency with those that are vibrating in the energy of love and support. Thus, I am vibrating at the frequency to call forth similar experiences. As I send sincere blessings to them for their completions, it also lifts my energy and allows me to get in touch with my dreams.

The more we surround ourselves with people that do not support our success, their very presence implants doubt in our minds, and that doubt begins to grow. People that are not at the same frequency are very similar to crabs in a bucket. Have you have ever observed a bucket full of crabs? When the crabs are all frantically scrambling and trying to escape, as one crab gets to the very top of the bucket and is almost ready to make its getaway, invariably one of the other crabs reaches up and pulls the escaping crab back in.

Being in the energy of those that have similar dreams gives energy to your vision also. As you focus on results instead of focusing on how, it creates the connection that aligns your desires.

> Surround yourself with high-energy people.
> Choose to be in close proximity to people who
> are *empowering*, who appeal to your sense of
> connection to intention, who see the greatness in
> you, who feel *connected* to God,
> and who live a life that gives evidence that
> Spirit has found celebration through them.
> -Wayne Dyer

We Know The Way

> One often meets their destiny on the
> way to somewhere else. At first
> glance it may appear too hard.
> *Look again* ... always look again.
> -Mary Anne Radmacher

I was spending the day in the mountains with a group of people. I decided to stay behind and spend some time in private meditation. I hiked around, enjoying the nature around me, then after a while I decided I should head home before it was too dark. On my way back I discovered the bridge I had to cross was unapproachable from where I was. I would have to back track for some time to get around a mud swamp.

In my heart, I knew the way I should take, but it was going to be quite a distance back around. It was getting late, and I was in a hurry to get out of the mountains. I figured I could easily go across the mud and save some time. I took a few steps in, and even though I began to think I was not making a good choice, in my hurry I blew the thought off and continued. I rationalized that I could just wash my shoes off in the river when I got across. As I stepped, I quickly found myself engulfed in mud to my chest, and there was no one around to help me.

At first I began to laugh, thinking how comical it was that I would be in this situation and have to go back and face people all covered in gunk. Soon the reality set in: This situation was serious. Every time I attempted to lift a foot, my shoe got stuck, and I would sink a little further under the mud.

The process continued for over an hour. The deeper I was sinking in the disgusting ooze that surrounded my body, the more I grasped the reality that this was not just a messy, awkward situation, I was actually in danger.

I was in the middle of the mountains submerged to my armpits in a mud pit. It was getting dark, and there was not a person around that could help me. Every movement I made, I sank deeper in the vastness of the pit.

I began to panic. I was envisioning the things that could happen, knowing that I would not even be missed for days because I was out of town, my friends I was planning to meet would just assume I wasn't showing up having left my commitment open ended. The humiliation of coming this far in my life to be engulfed by mud as my final demise was haunting. The stench was incredible and the feeling of every bend and crevice of my body surrounded by a warm goo was disgusting. Any attempted movement took me deeper into the abyss.

Exhausted, I finally quit resisting. Instead of fighting, I turned inward sincerely asking "Now what?" In that moment of surrender, the sun was setting, and one of the last rays of sunlight hit my eyes. My inner wisdom asked if I was going to choose to follow or keep

Beyond Beautiful

forcing my way through. My deep reflection brought me to the awareness of how many times I think I can just bulldoze through something and make it happen, using force to move forward.

A humbling spirit then reminded me that life doesn't have to be this hard; it is hard because I allow my ego to be in charge. "Be still and listen, the answers are right there inside you," was my only message. In that moment I relinquished my fight, and a tingling power of peace poured over me. I trusted my intuition that said, "lean into the experience."

Immediately, my ego mind again took over, thinking that was a ridiculous message. Here I am, deeply emerged in this disgusting stuff, and my answer is to "lean in"? My awareness enhanced that the situation was getting bleaker by the minute, I chose to trust and lean in to the mud.

Looking at the smelly, foul, gooey mud before me, I was ever aware of the pressure and tightness as the mud surrounded my whole body. I had been trying to get out of this mess through physical pressure and power, and I hadn't been able to get anywhere. Attempting to approach this the same way over and over as I had done, only kept me sinking deeper into the mud. I knew that soon the mud would consume me.

In my resignation, I laid down on top of the mud, placing the side of my face in the filthy stench. Instinctively, I put my arms outward like an airplane, laying in the disgusting ooze that completely engulfed my body, and I leaned in. My body slowly came up to the top of the mud.

I was beyond the mental dialogue, the questioning and the thoughts. I was in a complete space of trust that Spirit was showing me the way. Laying on top of the mud, I instinctively swam across. With the smell and stench of the mud ever present, I quickly arrived on dry ground covered in inches of smelly, disgusting muck from head to toe. I looked and smelled like a repugnant creature from a horror movie. But the joy that filled my soul was amazing. I chose to surrender and listen to my inner knowing, and I was alive on safe ground again!

How many times do we know the path that will take us to the place we desire, but go against our inner knowing, choosing the short cut, that compromises our choice? When you are in a situation in which you feel stuck, do you continue to do the same thing over and over again, expecting somehow the outcome will be different?

I learned that the moment I make the choice to quit resisting my experience, accept the fact that this is the situation I created, and trust my inner knowing to guide my next step, that I will always be safe. If I kept fighting against the situation, I was going to get deeper in the mess and continue to go under the mud, perhaps even to the point that it would kill me. As long as I continued to listen to my mind and the mental chatter going on within, I was on a downward spiral toward what I didn't want. As I gave up the fight and asked a higher power for guidance, I instinctively knew the answer to my freedom. The answer was there all along but my ego's attempt to be in charge prolonged my confinement.

Our ego is a gift to us when it is a servant to our Spirit. When it is the other way around, the identity of our ego and its desire to be in charge keeps us forever stuck, similar to a dog chasing its tail. In trusting my inner voice, I literally chose to live life. The most fascinating thing is that listening and following my intuition was something so easy and simple, that in a matter of a few minutes of following Spirit, I was on safe ground.

Our ego's desire is to have some grand answer or drama to resolve the problem. When the answer was something so easy as leaning into the experience instead of resisting it, every part of my ego wanted to say, "No! That won't work." Even though there were many reasons why I did not want to put my face in the gunk and float on top of the mud, leaning in was the answer to being safe.

Think of the times your intuition has told you something and you have dismissed it because it seemed too easy. If the answer feels too simple, it is probably the right one. We spend so much time attempting to make things complicated when solutions and movement can occur instantly by making a conscious choice to live instinctively.

Prayers Of Gratitude

{
If the only prayer you ever

say in your entire life

is *thank you*, it will be enough.

-Meister Eckhart
}

Every experience we have is a form of spiritual training. As experiences take us on a path that we are not expecting, embracing the situation and seeing the gift in what is presented always holds a higher level of learning. Thus, our greatest challenges in life are also our greatest teachers. Everything we experience brings a deeper level of awareness about who we really are.

While my children and I were in Australia for me to do an intense study and mentorship for my work in Neuro Energetic Kinesiology, my husband moved our family to another state where he resided. After living apart for over a year, I quickly realized our relationship was not fulfilling me. We divorced shortly after our move.

Because of my desire for my children's lives not to be more disrupted than they already had been, I decided to stay in our new home when my training in Australia ended. I absolutely hated being there. Previously, I lived at the base of the majestic Rocky Mountains, where every day I looked out my window to see the beautiful mountains, loving the nature that surrounded me. I could take the four wheelers up the mountains with my children to a pond, wildlife and trees.

My new residence was totally different with its brown, rolling hills and very few trees except along the river. This was devastating to me. There was nothing that brought me joy. I was all alone, I knew no one, I had left my friends and clients and now my marriage. I felt myself falling deeper and deeper into depression.

The rental house we were living in was much smaller than the house I had moved from. I had felt like I was in the depths of despair, having no interaction with people in my new life especially after letting go of a 23-year marriage that never worked for me.

Everything around me was ugly. I was doing my basic duties as a mother but there was nothing else I had in my life. I was overwhelmed with the prospects of rebuilding my business in a new city. I was completely isolated from the world and when my children were gone to school, I was left in the aloneness of myself.

My only solace was the pond in the back yard of the rental home. One night as I laid in bed with my window open, aware of the vast emptiness that surrounded me, I heard the sound of a frog: Ribbit! It was a deep bellow that brought a smile to my face. I remembered when my children were younger, there was a pond nearby where we would go every spring and catch pollywogs. We would bring them home and watch them grow into frogs, and then let them go when they were grown. This was one of our favorite experiences together and memories of this simple experience brought back happiness.

I began to listen for the "Ribbit!" of the frog every night. My deep gratitude for the songs the frog sang brought me a joy to look forward to. I uttered a prayer in my heart: Thank you for the frog that makes me happy. I began to anticipate the night, ever aware of the sounds in the pond. I noticed the ducks made a snoring sound. I was grateful for the sound of the ducks. I became aware of the sound of geese gliding across the water. I loved hearing their honking noises, which brought me a strength and knowing that everything will be okay.

My love for the pond and the wildlife continued to grow. The pond was my solace. Observing the animals simply celebrating life brought life back to me. The prayer in my heart for these small blessings grew. I focused more love and gratitude for the simplest things life gives us. My awareness of how much life supports us and gives bounteous gifts deepened my appreciation for the beauty of life.

I became conscious of all the gifts, no matter how small and

insignificant they may be, all were vibrating to their own expression of life. The expansion of my awareness of the dew on the grass, the hummingbird that buzzed outside my window, the squirrel that made his home in a tree in my yard, and simply driving past a small river with a huge willow tree beside it, made my life full. My gratitude for the small gifts in life gave me back my vivacity and reminded me of my ever present wholeness within. I opened my heart and loved all that was around me and life loved me back.

I learned that I could change many things in my world by being in gratitude for the small things life offers me. Gratitude for all of life is the key to opening our receptivity to more abundance. Giving gratitude for the things that I had previously taken for granted opened up a whole new flow of blessings in my life. Receiving the small gifts and in return giving love and gratitude back, created positive movement and restored my joy and love for life.

I expanded my appreciation for small gestures that I received from others. I learned that the more thankful I am for the blessings I have, the more avenues open for other kinds of miracles to occur. I learned that my prayer of gratitude for those small things in my life brought other opportunities for me to live. As I sincerely thanked Source for all I experienced, no matter how small the gift; abundance poured over me, giving me more opportunities.

My appreciation also expanded to learning to give to myself. I gave gratitude to myself for finding ways to love and nurture me. As I gave gratitude and love for what was in my life now, avenues of aliveness, growth, and fulfillment entered my being. My thankfulness expanded my power to create more love and abundance.

We sabotage our lives by believing our circumstances should be different. Blessing our experience brings us wisdom and gifts. Gratitude for what we already have expands our ability to receive. Standing in our own power and majesty, boldly claiming our heart desires, holds a space of contentment. Positively focusing on what is working quickly allows more positive energy to surround us. Gratitude is a spiritual practice that opens doors to all possibilities and shares an abundance of light, love and joy to others. Changing our perspective that something different has to occur to be grateful is the wrong approach. Feeling good now, enjoying the miracles that are ours and being thankful for all we do have, opens the doors of all good to flow to us. Knowing that you deserve the beauty of your dream gives energy to flourish. Focusing on the infinite power rapidly multiplies our gifts of success.

Saying Yes to Me!

> There are two *great days* in a person's life – the day we are born and the day we discover why.
>
> -William Barclay

Life's purpose is to remember who we are and to recognize our own unique soul essence and the beautiful mission we are to fulfill. As a divine, wise soul, all the wisdom and power is contained within. Standing in our strength, dismissing our fears and doubts, and living in integrity with our dreams is where all possibilities lie.

The greatest question to ask now is what do you want to experience? We are trailblazers, on a journey of breaking through our illusions and perceptions. We are in an ever-changing world which provides opportunities to learn deeper aspects of ourselves. When we come to realize that in this journey called life everything changes and nothing stays the same, then opportunities open for continual evolution. Learning the value of flexibility and freedom to live fully as we desire and aligning ourselves to our true values provides deeper meaning to not only ourselves but to our world.

By passionately following our dreams we open an incredible journey of adventure. We are the creator of our lives. We can fully embrace our beauty and passions. Learning to find balance in our comfort and challenge is the real answer to all we seek. By releasing our fears

and ego, it allows us to have a deeper introspection of who we really are, awakening the possibilities for more satisfaction and growth.

Challenging our expectations of how it has to be and enjoying the journey is where true happiness lies. There is not a destination in life, or a point at which we achieve what defines success. Most experiences turn out differently than imagined, but holding a space of love and light and being present in the moment, creates fulfillment in our love for life. Our continual quest for expansion and expression while trusting that we are perfect just as we are allows us to fully embrace the beauty and celebration of life.

Every day we must invest energy to grow, build and develop ourselves. This is the answer to embracing the life we love and desire. Imperative is the recognition of both our inner and outer beauty. We hold the key to unlock our inner radiance and light, letting it shine the true essence of love. Every experience in life is teaching us how to love on a deeper level. As we give ourselves permission to be our true self, our light ignites a flicker in others, giving them permission to fully be in their power of beauty. We all must take a stand for ourselves, creating a ripple of love that unites us in a thriving world of possibilities.

The truest form of love we can give someone is our own growth. In our aliveness and passion for purpose, we also give others permission to seize their own truth. By living in our highest purpose and power we inspire courage for others to be on their own path. As we follow yearnings of our heart, we are always on the route to success.

We can make a meaningful contribution to the world by living from the beauty within, from the part of ourselves that is beyond beautiful.

Robyn Podboy

Dedicated to everyone looking
to unlock the answers to
find their own happiness!

Chapter 4
Live Your Life In Laugher!

Chapter 4

Live Your Life In Laughter!

As long as I can remember, people have told me how much fun they have whenever we are together. How they have never really laughed that hard before, or that they just feel better when they are with me and can let their hair down. Somehow I am always surprised … Doesn't everyone have "that much" fun? Or, is the answer that I was able to give them "permission" to have their own fun? When my children were running out the door heading off for school, my husband would say, "study hard"; while I would say, "HAVE FUN!" Now, I think: "What's that about? Why did I always say that?"

I am not sure why I actually think in terms of life should be fun and full of laughter. I wanted to open up and look within to see what people were talking about and to feel what they felt when we were together. I wanted to shed light on the laughter in my life, and why it was so important to me.

Through the help of laughter, I have learned most of my life lessons. For me, laughter has been a crutch to lean on, a shield to hide behind, and a way to live my best life.

Here are a few of my stories I would like to share with the hope you will be inspired to find your light from within, to live your life in laughter and know you are meant to be happy!

Tears Of A Clown

When I was growing up I was always the kid who was afraid of not being popular, being left out, or worse yet, being made "fun of," which would have been a fate worse than death!

So from as far back as I can remember, I thought if I could "make fun" of myself before anyone else, I'd be safe. If I was funny, then maybe people would like me. I would hide behind my shield, and no one could hurt me. Laughing was my repellent to being hurt. Being able to see now all the damage I was creating, what I needed most was protection from MY thoughts, not what others would think or do.

When we are first born, we instinctively know how to laugh. Seeing little babies laugh out loud or smile makes everyone around them laugh and smile! Babies, at least initially, know how to "live in laughter," and their first laugh comes straight from the heart.

Having a lot of fun in my house with my parents is not one of my childhood memories. Dad was always yelling at us for something we did or didn't do. "Wipe your feet" ... "Don't slam the door!" Mom was always walking on egg shells. Feeling the frustration from both my parents in the life they had chosen, the atmosphere in our house always felt heavy! Far, far away from any fun.

Our dinner table epitomized the family battle zone and each member's role in the family. Mom was always the perfect "people pleaser." Dad was, crabby, ill and unhappy. My older brother had a tongue that would cut you til you bled. I was the actress and joke teller, making fun of everything, sometimes in a dramatic way. My little brother never said much at the table, he knew better.

Dinner table time was our "family time," and it was the mirror of our misery. Every night there was drama around some ridiculous situation that would start out seemingly innocent enough. But, with every bite of food, the tension and drama would build. We were never asked about our day, or what we learned at school. Absolutely no words were ever uttered in terms of having fun! After all, who has fun?

Trying to make polite conversation and appear interested, we would ask my father how his day went. "Rough," he would respond. Every single night "Rough" was always his answer. Every single night!! My older brother and I would then compete for the spotlight of conversation, and after someone would say a word or two …. Ding, ding let the fights begin!

Dinner usually ended with me saying something inappropriate, then turning into the drama queen and running off crying to my room telling everyone how I hated them and wished they were dead. "Oh, Robyn, she is so fun," I used to say. Yeah, right. My life was such fun. "Tears of a Clown" by Smokey Robinson ... that was me... but nobody knew the real me.

Smile Though Your Heart is Breaking

Many times in my life, I would smile, laugh and hide behind the shield in order to make it through my heartbreak. Smile! Be happy! … while inside you feel as if your heart is being ripped out of your chest. There was an incident when I was in second grade where I hid behind my shield, and for the first time, I realized that the "shield" was an instinctive reaction that helped me survive!

The day of our Christmas Class Party for my second grade class, the buzz was in the air! We had made decorations for the room and our desks, and even had a real Christmas tree in the corner. The party was set to begin as soon as our room-mother arrived with all the goodies and drinks. Oh, the anticipation!!

Our room-mother was the mom of the most popular girl in the class. I'll never forget Mrs. Rudolph ... (Kind of funny isn't it, her name being Rudolph, and she was bringing the goodies to the Christmas party) … anyway, I'll never forget Mrs. Rudolph as she walked into our room with her hands full of all the goodies and drinks.

But wait! Something had happened to her and everyone was a little freaked out at her appearance. She had a huge, white, gauzy band aid covering her entire nose and stuffing in her nostrils! Everyone was asking simultaneously, "Oh what happened? What happened to you, Mrs. Rudolph?" We were all sitting at our desks waiting to

Beyond Beautiful

hear the answer.

Suddenly, it seemed to me as if everything was occurring in slow motion. Her arms seem to extend longer… her fingers seemed to stretch, turn green and furry just like the Grinch's. She was saying out loud… as loud as a bell … "HER father hit me … with his car … and he … BROKE MY NOSE!" Oh my gosh, was she really pointing at ME? I could feel this burn in my heart … I think my heart was crying deep within me! I couldn't breathe.

Mrs. Rudolph was laughing, and all the kids in the class had turned and were now staring incredulously at me…. I could feel the heat in my face which turned twenty shades of red. But I just smiled and quietly said under my breath that I hoped that her new nose would be a whole lot smaller …

Wow!! This is one fun party, huh? … Okay, class! Now, let's have a goodie!

As I grew older and was meeting mean girlfriends and even meaner boyfriends, I would hide behind my shield many, many times … and the fun continued …

When I was a child I'd have the most "fun" at my Aunt Ann's house with my four cousins. We would make up insane games that turned out to be the "times of my life." They became the foundation of how to fill my life with laughter. My aunt always let us kids be … well, kids. She taught us how to have "fun," to be happy with what life has to offer. If you can't find it … you make it.

Embracing the new day, we would hear a "good morning" song being sung in a high pitched voice to wake us up! So, our days would start out with a laugh because she just sounded so God-awful! If she didn't sing to us, we would wake to the sound of her own laughter. Maybe it was something the dog did or something she heard on the TV. But the day always started with a giggle.

Every Christmas Eve would be spent down in her basement playing "Murder in the Dark," a card game which we had all made up. In this game, if your card was the Ace of any suit you were the killer …

with the lights out.

We would walk around like zombies, and if you were touched by the killer you must scream as loud as you could and fall to the ground. I know it sounds simplistic, but we were kids …. and it was FUN!

Meanwhile the adults were upstairs drinking highballs, listening to the music of Bing Crosby, celebrating the holiday … all the while with the sounds of blood-curdling screams coming from the basement. They usually let us have "our" fun, and there were only a few times when the screaming became so loud they couldn't hear the Christmas music, then they asked us to "keep it down"!

Every year for my older cousin's birthday, we would take the train down to the city to see a play at the Goodman Theater in Chicago. This trip would be just for me, my cousin and my aunt. It was over the top! We dressed up in our nicest dresses and took the train to downtown Chicago! How FUN!

We would sit on the upper deck of the train across from each other and talk in gibberish. We made up a whole new language on the spot, having a whole conversation the entire trip down to the city. We laughed until we cried thinking of how funny we sounded to the others on the train. We were ridiculous, having fun and full of joy! My aunt would just smile, then off to the theater we would go.

Decorating Christmas cookies each year with my aunt and cousins, the boys would always put inappropriate sparkles and silver balls on them. They would most definitely put you into a sugar coma if you dared to actually eat one, or you'd for sure break a tooth! Laughing at our artistic nature, never worrying about what others would think, my aunt would laugh and say we were crazy idiots; but she never criticized! In her eyes, we were all Rembrandts.

At my aunt's house, we would do all sorts of crazy and fun things. We'd try riding our bikes backwards only to crash and lose a tooth or scrape a shin. Climbing trees someone would break an arm, or sprain something. We'd go on camping trips and get lost. We would ride my in my uncle's dune buggy around the neighborhood like we were in the Macy's parade.

One of our favorite games was the "making goop game" where we would mix any kind of ingredient found from the pantry... mix it together in a bowl, blindfold each victim, then spoon feed them. They would have to guess what was in the mixture. Many times (most always), it would end up with at least one of us throwing up … Oh yes! We could "play" at their house. Is it any wonder it was one of my favorite places in the world to be??

Humor is the beginning of wisdom. The best times in life are when you are laughing because this is when you are connected with your soul... It feels true. It feels right!

Pomp And Circumstance

Many people in my family have suffered with depression, and I was one of them. I recognize the times in my life when I have been depressed, and my thoughts were lost. Hiding behind the Tears of a Clown was so exhausting that when no one was around I would give myself permission to feel the pain of my sadness ... I would get lost in my feelings.

It was so easy to turn on "the clown" and wear "that shield." I felt fake one minute and grateful the next. I didn't always have to be "on." Sometimes I would spend hours in my room rearranging the furniture or cleaning out my closet and yes, probably painting a new color on the wall. I can see how this helped me sort out, clean out, and change my thoughts. Somehow this always seemed to help me feel better about whatever was going on at the time.

I was not one of those lucky students in school who found that one awesome teacher who was interested in me or truly inspired me. My teachers were sarcastic, condescending and felt personally insulted if I didn't understand something. They never felt it had anything to do with their teaching style, but rather it was because I just was unable to "get it." It became easier for most teachers to just pass me to the next grade instead of giving me the extra help that I needed.

But one year they didn't just pass me, and I was held back in third grade unable to go on to fourth grade. They thought if I had third grade over again maybe this time I'd "get it." There was nothing I could do to make fun of this situation ... so, I hid behind my shield. My parents decided to take me out of my current school and enroll me in a private Christian school. They hoped that maybe I wouldn't get teased from old classmates, and that this change wouldn't be so hard on me. This new Christian school was in the next town over from ours. I was told that Dad would drive me to the "church school," since it was on his way to work. The plan was that after school, I'd go to a different girl's house every day until he could pick me up on his way home from work ... this made for a long day!

I really didn't want to go to "the church school," because after all, I barely enjoyed going to church there! During this time in my little life, I felt so alone and scared. Was I really repeating third grade? I felt like a stupid loser who couldn't learn. It was during this time period that my low self-esteem and feelings of unworthiness really solidified. I developed that "lost" feeling.

Because Dad had to be to work at the same time school started, I would be dropped off early before they'd actually opened the doors to the building. I'd have to sit on the front steps and wait. A girl who lived across the street frequently came early, too. At first I thought she'd be my friend, and we could have fun together while we waited for school to start, but it didn't take long for me to realize that her idea of fun was to torment ME.

Every day it would be a different kind of torture and anguish. Sometimes, she would hide behind bushes making fun of my clothes or short hair, or letting me know just how stupid and dumb I was. I believed everything she said wholeheartedly. After all, I WAS stupid... for coming to this school!

I don't remember having any conversations with my dad on the way to or from this school during that whole year. What I do remember is smiling on the outside and crying on the inside, thinking: "Please don't drop me off and leave me!!" I would bargain with him in my mind: "I'll do anything you want me to do!! I won't fight with my

brother or say funny, inappropriate things! I'll be quiet and small ....
Just please don't leave me -- oh no, he's gone ... PLEASE just come
back and get me! Please!!" But Dad's car never turned around ...

One day at the church school the snow began to fall. I couldn't
seem to pay attention to anything the teacher was saying. That was
actually the norm for me; but this day, I just kept watching the snow
fall from my classroom window. So quiet and beautiful. It snowed
all through the day, and there was a rumor going around that we
could possibly be released early from school because the roads were
getting bad. The excitement built, and soon it was true. We were
released early!

This was on a Thursday, which meant that I would be staying at
Eileen Houlihan's house until Dad could pick me up. She lived
across the street from the school so we just walked home together
in the deep, wonderful snow!! Yeah! I couldn't wait to get out
there and play in it! As we trudged up to the door, Eileen's mom
greeted us by saying that it would be "best" if we came inside and
just watched the snow fall. What?? All this beautiful snow, and we
can't play in it?? But Mrs. Houlihan wasn't ready to deal with the
wet mess and besides, as she pointed out ... I "didn't have any snow
pants!"

I couldn't wait till my dad could pick me up because I knew my
brothers would be out playing in this great snow, and when I got
there, we would have a blast! As it grew darker then became time
for dinner, I knew that my dad wasn't going to come get me to take
me home.

I was told that the roads were too bad so I "get to stay" with the
Houlihans. Oh Yippee... the fun Houlihans that don't like the snow!
I felt like Dorothy from the Wizard of Oz... I just wanted to go home
... the voice in my head tugged at me and told me that I wasn't
worth the effort for anyone to come and get me.

I was stranded at the Houlihan's house until that following Monday.
As each day passed, I couldn't wait til it was time for bed so then
I could cry into my pillow and try to make time pass quickly. The
newspapers called this storm the "Blizzard of the Century!" I

128

witnessed the whole thing FROM INSIDE THE HOUSE and got to play in it once, for a "whole" half an hour, because after all, I "didn't have any snow pants!!"

It was very hard for me to hide behind my shield of smiling on the outside and crying on the inside... FOR FOUR DAYS!

When I turned 15, I started working at my first job. I was so proud of my REAL job. My work place became an important place for me because I felt loved and appreciated. I found out that I was good at something, and I could learn anything I wanted to learn. I was proud of myself and my accomplishments for the first time in my life. I could have fun without hiding behind my shield. I had great friends, found boyfriends and loved the funny me!

This was also the time in my life that I found out why there was always so much tension between my parents, and why my father seemed so unhappy all the time. During a self-induced fight with him, I defiantly asked, "Why don't you have a happy life? Why are you so miserable?"

He did, in fact, have a blast in his life before I knew him. He was a great looking guy with tons of friends. He was the life of every party. He was funny, sweet, fun to be around. Playing Bass in his band, he loved music and dancing. Laughter was a big part in his life. Actually, it sounded like we could have been friends! We were very much the same, except I was not in a band, and he was not was a girl!

Our fight gathered speed and increased in intensity as he spat out the words like old rotten teeth: "YOUR MOTHER HAD AN AFFAIR." I was stunned. What did he say?? My mother had an affair?? Oh my gosh, my mother had an affair! Then another bombshell: My little brother was not his child, but he had to "put up with this charade."

He was hiding behind a shield of his own, but not very well. All this had changed him into a lost and defeated man. He felt alone, and he felt broken. Suddenly the pieces were falling together and it was

starting to make sense …. Well sort of….

I wanted to know all the details but, that would take years. When the whole truth came out, I found out that his wounds ran deep. Mom's affair was with his best friend, and he became the joke of our neighborhood. After that day of our fight, he never talked about it again!

I handled this newfound knowledge as I did with everything. I'd make fun of it before anyone else could. Shield myself from it. Laugh at it and cry on the inside. I tried to figure out how this could happen. This now became my story of betrayal. I hated my parents because of what they had done to each other and to us as a family. I started to fantasize how life would have been different, how we could have been a family that had fun together … I was convinced of that!

But the one thing I knew absolutely without question: I loved my little brother. I didn't care where he came from, I was just glad that he was mine. We would spend hours together making up commercials to recite in the mirror, playing school, (I was the mean teacher, of course). We were inseparable! We wore the same shield. We thought the same things were funny. We both knew each other very well. I wanted to protect him.

After the fateful day of the argument, I started to own this lie and betrayal as if it was mine own. I carried the burden of our family secret. Did anyone outside our family know?

Ah .. now it makes sense …. Is that why we never did anything together as a family? Ah yes…. I felt like I was wearing a heavy jacket of lies, and I needed to understand all of the truth before I could take it off.

I found that being with my friends and away from my family was easier for me. That way, I didn't have to witness their unhappiness first-hand. Everything at home was a constant reminder of lies and betrayal, even though it was not mine. I started to betray myself by doing drugs, having sex, giving up on going to school all together, and starting my own set of lies. I was having so much fun, that in the

fun I was having, I was not having any fun at all …

I was able to graduate from high school, but not because of any wisdom or help from a teacher or a parent. I made the effort to graduate from high school because I didn't /couldn't miss the FUN of wearing a cap and gown, then walking down to receive my diploma at graduation to the strains of "POMP AND CIRCUMSTANCE" playing! Oh, that "Pomp and Circumstance" song … Couldn't miss that!

Pushing to pass all the classes I needed to accomplish this, I was relying on myself and a few teachers I begged for extra credit. I remember what my counselor told my mother at the graduation ceremony … "We need to have a drink!" Are you kidding me? I'M the one who needs a drink!

It has taken me years to understand that my parents were doing the best they knew how to do. The decisions that they made in their marriage were their choices! They chose not to seek counseling; they chose not to talk through the pain. THEIR CHOICES!

I needed to understand that this was not my pain. This was not my burden to carry or to try and fix. I had been accepting their pain on top of my own pain. This emptiness I was feeling was impossible to fill because it was THEIRS not MINE! I didn't need to hide behind my shield, do drugs, find love in bad relationships or even try to fill it up with cookies!

I needed to forgive them and to forgive myself. To let it go… I have a choice! Bingo!

Once I was able to forgive and understand that this was their own journey... in their own life …. that I had my own journey with my own choices … that I could decide … when I focused on my own pain … when I stopped trying to fix "it," then I slowly took off my shield and finally I could feel safe in just a t-shirt!

Twenty Colleges

College was actually Time-on-the-Job Training (TOJ) for me. I have had at least twenty different jobs in my life. Some I have had for many years while others I have had for a few days. All of these different jobs gave me my life experience that no college could have done for me. Remember I was not the best student. But, when I went into the workforce I gave it my all. I worked for each employer as though this was my new career, this was my newest passion! With the experience of having so many different jobs, my resume grew along with my self-knowledge.

Most of the jobs were a "dream job" at that time in my life. Each one seemed to prepare me for the next adventure or the next trial of my life. I was learning so much about myself and the world, it was like I had attended twenty colleges!

I can reflect on each experience with a lot of laughter now, although some of my learning experiences were not funny at all at that time. I took each one them very seriously. Not feeling as "educated" as most of the world that did go to college, my self-esteem issues would kick in at parties or during a conversation with the inevitable question: "Where did you go to college?" Ah..Ah…. I would always answer with the colleges I had " partied" at. Then I didn't feel like I was lying.

For me it is unimaginable not to have fun in the workplace. If I was going to spend most of my time there, I was going to work hard and also make it a fun place to be. I remember someone saying once that I would probably get fired for too much laughter and unbelievably, that really did happen once!

I have many stories about the different jobs and people I have met in each one, but I'll pick just one to share with you. I hope that it will give you a feel for me in the workplace.

Diets have been a part of my life since I was in about sixth grade. I remember my first meal from that very first diet: A tuna melt with a garden green salad topped off with green goddess salad dressing.

This was it!! I was going be as thin as Twiggy! At this time I did not have a weight problem, I had a low self-esteem problem! But, this was the beginning of what would become my yo-yo diet way of life. Every day as I woke up, my very first thought was to start another diet or exercise program. I would try to find a quick fix or magic pills, read a new book, join the latest gym, or weight loss center. This was my constant topic at parties, at work, with family members, even people that I didn't even know. I'd see that they were thin, ask them how they were staying so slim.

I knew to stay consistent and be successful with my weight loss goal which was always changing, I must find something fun to do! So what did I enjoy doing? I enjoyed tennis, running, walking. Aha! The answer!! But I soon found that the enjoyment did not last. Before long, when it was no longer "fun" for me, I just stopped doing these things!

Then I tried to make the "dieting" a fun process, too. I joined a weight loss center with a friend. Doing this together, we were going to be consistent, and this would be just the skinny ticket I needed! It's fun to wait, stand in line, and hop on a scale to be weighed! Oh, we could hardly wait to have fun! Every week we would stand on that scale to only lose .25 lbs. Yes, POINT-TWO-FIVE pounds!! One quarter of a pound! That is the equivalent to one stick of butter. That's IT!

We would return to the car, look at each other and cry. I mean literally CRY. Why was this so hard for us and not others? We made dishes from recipes and shared ideas with each other. The women we attended this meeting with were losing weight and found this program was working for them. THEY were having fun!!
This was the most successful weight loss franchise in the world, and we were only losing .25 lbs. a week!! The tears were flowing like a river. After our meltdown, the tears turned to laughter at the absurdity of how we were reacting to our .25 lb. weight loss. We could not control the laughter at the "Patty pity party" we just gave ourselves.

That moment was a turning point, I stopped making excuses and started to take responsibility to lose the weight to feel better

about myself. I realized that I thought that just because I joined the program I would automatically start losing weight. I mean, after all, I paid for it!

I was the yo-yo dieter, playing teeter-totter with my weight, going up and down until I hit my 40's. Then once I turned 40, I had become the Yo dieter. Yo meaning I wasn't going up and down anymore, I was just going up!

When we moved to a new city for my husband's job yet again, the stress of this move put me into the arms of my new best friend: Mr. Refrigerator. I needed to find a new life here, and, of course, lose weight. As I was searching the web looking for the job of my dreams, I found it: Working for a weight loss center that needed counselors/sales representatives. Perfect!! That is SO me! I could help people lose their unwanted weight, help them live a happy, thin life and maybe in the process I will actually help myself, too! Hurray! I knew there was a reason we moved to this town!

While working there, I met some wonderful co-workers, and our clients were a sea of variety. Every day I was helping people move to the direction of a happier life through weight loss. At the time I was hired I thought it was a combination of sales and counseling but it really was a sales job assisting them with purchasing programs, supplements, etc.

I believe our center was different than most, mainly due to my co-workers. I never had to sell clients anything that I felt they didn't need or wouldn't use. I loved spending a lot of time working with each client helping them make the right choices in their life which would make them choose to be happier.

One of the things I did was create "theme days" so that when each client would come to the center they would enter an atmosphere that was positive and happy. Most clients wouldn't want to miss what "the girls" at the center where doing today!

On St. Patrick's Day I played Irish music all day and spoke in an Irish brogue: "Top of the morning to ya!" On April Fool's Day when the client would come to "weigh in," I'd take them back to the scale so

we could record their weight. While I would weigh them, one of my co-workers would stand behind them and put HER foot on the scale. Without a doubt they would see a weight gain! "That just can't be true" … April Fool's Day!! Laughter would bounce from the walls. At the end of each day I had made weight loss fun!

I was helping people understand and accept the importance of themselves, to know that they were worthy! Their self-esteem was low, but I would help them recognize their worthiness in all areas of their lives, not just their weight loss commitment.

I, too, needed to feel the worthiness within myself. I won't lie to you, this is still challenging for me, and the teeter-totter of self-esteem is something I work on every day. It has nothing to do with whatever certain weight that I am. It's about being happy with myself just the way I am. When I am feeling in love with myself or really liking myself, the weight seems to let go. When I am feeling out of love with myself, I am totally out of balance. This is my teeter totter.

I stayed at the weight loss center for a couple of years until I felt that the company was pressuring us to sell unethically, and I had to leave. The other girl there said that I was the one that made it really fun to work there, but I think we were meant to be there to work together. It was our chemistry that made it so fun!

One of the co-workers went through a very abusive divorce during the time I was there. She has since shared with me that being able to come to work and live in laughter helped her through the most difficult time in her life. She was helping others and in return helped herself! When you change the way you see yourself... You see yourself change!

Oh just in case you want to know, I did lose about 25 lbs., and I gained a ton of knowledge!

Laugh 'til the Cows Come Home

Friends come in and out of our lives for many reasons: To grow, to help us learn, to enjoy life, and, of course, to have fun with. The friendship I want to tell you about was an eye opening lesson for me reflecting to me the type of person I did not want not to be! I am grateful to have had this mirror so I could change and become who I wanted to be.

Together my friend and I spent countless hours gossiping and making fun of others. You name it, I made fun of it! We would speculate about their families, what they were thinking, what they were doing, who they were with, etc. having a wonderful time laughing at the expense of others. My behavior was ugly (as they say down south), hateful, and so mean, but at the time I thought nothing of it! This was really funny stuff to me.

Every time I was with this friend, I found that I would engage in this kind of behavior. I would be weak, stooping to an ever lower level of this mean-ness humor. I did not like myself when I was around her. This wasn't the best of me; it was the worst of me. I had become that mean girl who used to torment me on the church school steps before school every morning! I couldn't believe this was how I chose to have fun.

I wanted to change my way of having fun but this was hard for us to do together. I would say to myself, "Today I will not gossip or say sarcastic, mean-spirited things when I speak of someone else," only to slide down to that lower level every time. But when I started to become aware of my behavior and wanted to change it, I found it impossible to listen to her talk because she was always so hateful and mean. How could I have not noticed before? I felt as if I was looking in the mirror…yuck!

I started working on being more of who I wanted to be, and learning how to have fun without being so hateful. Fortunately, my husband's job transferred us to another state. So, with the move, it was easier to let go of that friendship, and eventually the phone calls stopped.

After the move, I found that my sense of humor had changed, and what I found funny wasn't mean-spirited. I found that the craziness of life was hilarious enough, and I found humor in everything. Life was meant to be funny and to have fun in it! The people who came into my life felt the same as I did. Together we could laugh and have

fun without being mean!

I was shining in my own light. I discovered that living my life in laughter brought out the best in me, and I could be the person I truly wanted to be in the image of myself. I felt prettier, more alive, more connected to myself, and I am grateful to have the joy it brings into my life.

I found laughter to be the prosperity of my life! People have said to me, "Gosh you can get away with saying anything because you say it in a humorous way. I could never get away with that!" My response is always: "Yes you can – if you aren't being mean spirited or hurtful~ you will know the difference!"

Let Your Hair Down and Have Fun!

I love hanging out with my cousin, Phil. (Phil is one of my Aunt Ann's children.) We have recently re-connected, and our friendship has been awakened. Previously, we would see each other only occasionally at family reunions and at funerals. But whenever we would be together we would "get out of hand" (as most of the family would say)!

We always find ourselves laughing and telling stories, even making them up as we go along, just so we could laugh. We always laugh and carry on in an absurd way. We feed off each other's humor like ping pong, back and forth which makes our time together one big laugh fest. We feel alive!

We aren't being mean or ugly, we are just making this hilarious conversation. Sometimes, we even shock ourselves at the things that come out of our mouths. I think it must be channeled from a higher place! We only see each other once a year or so, both looking forward to our time together. Nothing is off limits, all of it is crazy fun – and laughter is good for our soul. Even our phone conversations can have long lasting effects that will bring a sudden burst of laughter when I think back on our crazy conversation. Now, this is what I'm talking about!

When I am in the true state of joy and laughter, I am in my bliss. The joy of this laughter can be contagious. When you carry that lightness of happy joy around you, people want to be a part of it! It's the warmth of the sunshine! The best time in life is when you are laughing. This is when you are connected with your soul! You can feel it and people see your shine!

> { As we let our own *light shine*, we unconsciously give other people permission to do the same.
> ~ Marianne Williamson }

I love being silly, letting my hair down and HAVING FUN! I love to sing at the top of my lungs in the car. I love crying and laughing in the same sentence. I love to dance like a hip hopper or like Elaine from "Seinfeld." I love talking using different voices and accents. I love singing karaoke! I love "being an idiot," as my aunt would say. The word" silly" is instant fun!

Recently I was at a workshop in San Diego. After a day of intense emotional work, a bunch of us decided to go out for dinner together even though none of us knew each other prior to this workshop. We went to the old town section to find an awesome authentic Mexican restaurant and have a nice margarita.

When we arrived, the restaurant was busy with lots of customers, but we got a table right away. As soon as we sat down, one of the girls in our group saw a man-clown going from table to table making balloon hats for those that wanted one. Jokingly she said that we needed to have one! So before we even looked at the menu, man-clown was at our table making all of us our balloon hats.

Eating dinner was a real challenge because we wanted to talk and have a conversation, but we couldn't be taken seriously with the hats on our heads. We were laughing like kids at a birthday party, and the laughter was contagious. Everyone around us found the energy intoxicating. Many said "Hey, I want to eat at your table," or "Boy, you guys sure know how to have fun!!" The looks we got from the children at the other tables were priceless. Most had their

mouths open in astonishment!

Our little group bonded tightly together over a night of being silly. The next day at the workshop, the hats were modeled for the large group before class began, and the room was lit with joy and laughter. See, contagious …

The next evening, our group from the night before went out together again, only this time with a few more friends. While walking on the boardwalk looking for a restaurant, out of the blue I saw an old time Carousel. "OH!" Without hesitation, I ran to it, my friends followed, each jumping on our favorite horse and away we all went.

When we jumped on to ride the carousel, not a soul was around. But by the time we were finished with the ride, a huge line had started to form to buy tickets for their turn. Our laughter and our singing attracted people to us. They started taking our pictures and waving to us; they wanted to ride the carousel; they wanted to have that much fun! We spent days laughing at ourselves and how it made us feel – We felt alive! We felt authentic. We were shining in that light of joy, and it was contagious!

My mom and her three sisters have that same sort of contagious kind of energy. When they are together having lunch, they are often asked to "keep it down" (meaning the laughter and noise). Sometimes they even fear they will be kicked out! There is nothing more inviting than a group engaged in laughter, you can't help but, smile!

Singing in the Rain

Having fun with my children brought out the kid in me! When they were young, my husband and I decided that I would be a stay-at-home mom to raise our two boys. We went through many sacrifices without a lot of money as a result of this decision. Since we lived far away from family, we depended on each other – we were all that we had.

I had always wanted to be a Mom… this was the job for me!! Playing and creating is one of my real joys in life. We would start and end

our days in play. But, it didn't start out this way.

Out of all of my friends in my area, I was one of the first to have a baby. After the excitement of planning and all the baby showers, and of course THE BIRTH, I wasn't prepared for the isolation from my friends. They were still in the partying scene while I was now a mom. My friends that did have kids lived in different locations, so I did not have a support group of moms. Looking in the paper one time for a "mommy and me" class, all I found was support groups for widowers or Alzheimer's. I felt as if I was totally on my own. Since we lived in an area where retired folks would come down for half the year, a group of young mothers was hard to find.

At times I felt overwhelmed, lonely for sure and depressed. I had always wanted this life: kids, diapers, toys, and bath time. I was lost in mommy-hood. I wasn't sure how to even BE a mom, let alone a good one. I felt the working moms seemed to have it going on. They could do both and not be isolated. I needed to find a balance in the mommy-hood so my days could be happy for me and my kids.

I went to see a family counselor who helped me realize that I had a choice of the kind of day that I wanted to have. I had made the choice to stay home. When I began to see what this freedom gave to me, I started to appreciate and be grateful for my life. I filled my days with fun for my kids.

Not to say that we didn't have stressful days, because we did. I would sometimes cry in my closet because I really hated that Barney song or the Jungle Book movie that was being requested yet again after already being watched over and over and over and over! But, after I realized that I had a choice whether I saw my days as fun or stressful, the stressful days became more infrequent. My outlook was now with a different set of eyes. Realizing that I truly had a choice became very powerful to me.

We would spend our days playing. My kids were able to just be a kid, making cookies, reading books, imagination play, building forts, watching movies on the couch. We would shop or go to the beach. When it rained we would run outside to splash in the puddles, and we'd be singing in the rain. This was how I wanted it to be!! I'm glad

that I did stay at home; I wouldn't have wanted it any other way. This was my best job ever, and I was good at it!

Bringing out the boys' humor was great fun for me. To see them as infants they seemed to laugh and already know what was funny to them. For example, they thought our dog, Dudley, was hilarious. Any time he was around with them, they would start this belly laugh that was contagious. Infants aren't taught to laugh, they just do! My boys copied my smile.

I would watch what was funny to them, and it was amazing to see they each had their own "sense of humor." I love that, their sense of humor. Where does that come from? Are we born with it? Why are some things funny to some and not to others?

I loved going to Second City in Chicago whenever I was in town, because it was fun just to laugh. I know that the comedians loved me in the audience because they could just walk onto stage, and I would start laughing. It was the anticipation of someone just about to tickle you.

I would play crazy games with the boys in anticipation of what might come next. One of their favorites was: "Mean Old Lady." I would sit on the couch reading a magazine, not paying attention to them as they would to walk by me. Sometimes I would grab them and throw them on the couch speaking in an old lady voice, "What are you doing walking by me?" Or, I would say, "I told you not to look at me that way!" Or "Why didn't you call me yesterday, Buddy?"

As I would fling them on the couch, they would dive into the cushions laughing hysterically. If I didn't grab them, they would walk really slowly in the anticipation of being flung into the cushions. It was a blast for them and for me. Some of the one-liners of why I was flinging them into the cushions made me laugh out loud, too. Then it was their turn to do it to me. It was the anticipation of not expecting fun that was so exciting.

One year when we lived in Atlanta, we surprised them by packing up the car while they were watching Sunday morning cartoons. Since my husband traveled it was not a big deal to have luggage

being hauled to the car. While we were having breakfast, we asked them to guess where we were going to go today to have fun? The clue was: "Where every kid wants to go. It's warm there, and it will take us hours to arrive."

One of the boys yells out: "Bowling?!!!" The other yells out: "A Braves game!!?" "Nope," we yell out, "Disneyworld!!!" " Now?" they screamed. "Yes Now!!! Let's jump in the car and go!" This memory they still cherish, because it was the anticipation of the fun we were going to have. It still brings us laughter today, not only because of the wonderful time we had together, but because of my youngest yelling out: "Bowling?!!!"

Even now when I'm with my boys, we still have fun laughing, enjoying each other's company and our unique sense of humor. They both have great wit with a wonderful outlook on life and the humor they find in it. They love to play, and it shows in everything they do. For this I am grateful!

Leaning on Laughter

Using laughter is scary, and what seems to be inappropriate times can be the saving grace for some.

When my childhood friend, Gail, and I were in our early 30's, she was unexpectedly diagnosed with leukemia, which was devastating for everyone hearing the news. She had so much life left to live, and there was this fear that she would die. At the time, I was living in Florida with my husband and two small children. Meanwhile she was in Chicago surrounded by all of her friends and family who were "getting in" on the drama of her cancer. Everyone around her were now experts on leukemia. This was very scary and helpless for all involved.

She had been my childhood friend who knew the secret of making fun, of wearing the shield of laughing at life when it puts you into a tough situation. Few of the people that surrounded her would participate with her in this outrageous behavior. There is NO laughing when you have cancer!! How could you be so ridiculous!

Trying to get through to speak with her on the phone was close to impossible, with all the people visiting and all that she was going through. She even had an answering machine on her hospital bedside phone! But when I did get to speak to her, we would spend our time laughing about this situation – even on her "bad" days.

We would speculate how all her blood transfusions could change her looks, or the way she'd be talking when she came out of this. We laughed at all the drama that surrounded her, including the "I'm a better friend than you" competition that was going on between her current girlfriends. Wow! The competition was fierce! Gail laughed and said it made her feel loved. We made fun laughing at all the gifts she was receiving from me because I couldn't be there with her. Everyday something new would be delivered by the hottest UPS guy to help make her comfortable or laugh. She was enjoying that part of the day!

After many months I was finally able to visit her. As I walked down the white hospital corridors slightly peeking into the rooms to see if I found her, I didn't even recognize her as I passed her room. There was an old lady in her room! I must have the wrong room number because I didn't see Gail, I saw a small woman with little scraggly white hair sprouting from her head and with black rings under her sunken eyes. This could not be Gail!

I had a bottle of champagne under my coat. Our tradition whenever one of us would pick each other up from the airport for a visit would be to have a bottle of champagne in the back seat with 2 glasses for an instant toast to the good time we were about to have! This was no different. As my husband and I entered the room, I instantly washed away the old lady in the bed that I had noticed before. I just saw the real Gail! Happy to finally be able to see each other, we popped open the champagne to celebrate!

We toasted to her, this crazy journey she was on and how strong she never thought she was. She had more tests in the morning, so the champagne was out for her. The nurses on her floor came in to see what was going on with all this laughter? We shared the champagne with a toast to them and their compassion! They said thanks to us for " this kind of visit" because laughter is the best medicine and this was just what she needed!! When Gail's tests were complete, she came home two days later!

She is not one for prayers, and her view on life is a pessimistic one. But, I do believe what helped her in the most difficult time of her life was the ability to find something funny about her situation, then tap into that to help make it manageable. Today, she is healthy, a beautiful wife, and a mother of two lovely daughters. Gail is living the life that back then, she could not have imagined.

Many years ago, the daughter of a close friend of mine was suddenly killed after work one night in a freak accident just right outside of her home. The daughter was in her early 20's, and the whole situation just tore out your heart with unbelievable grief.

In shock, I immediately drove from my home in NC to their home in Georgia. My feeling was that I had to be with my friend to try to help her with her grief and to help myself from feeling my own pain from this horrible experience. I needed to hug her!

When I got there it was very emotional and very difficult to have a moment together with so many people coming by the house, but we finally got to have that hug. Everyone was crying, greeting each other with hugs, and we began to talk and reminisce about the crazy funny things her daughter said or did in her life. We each enjoyed sharing our personal stories as our tears turned into laughter until the tears of joy were robust in the room. As more people started to arrive to give the family their condolences, I saw disapproving horror on their faces to see smiles and hear joyous laughter in such a time of grief. I could hear them silently thinking: "How can you laugh at a time like this?"

After returning home my friend wrote me a letter thanking me for helping everyone to remember to laugh. Her daughter was a fun seeker with a beautiful smiling face! Having a moment to laugh, in a situation that was so impossible to bear, lightened their hearts. They were remembering the day in that light!

Grieving and Growing

I didn't realize how much a person could learn in one year ... one painful year! One year, it seemed as if my world was going through a major shift. I've heard it said that when you go through a time in your life that is painful, this is a time of the most growth. Well, that year I grew tremendously!

When I met Julie we became fast and furious friends. We were working for a cruise company based in Chicago. I was running the cruises in Florida, and she was running the cruises in Chicago. We hadn't met in person before and only spoke on the phone. She was coming down to Florida to get out of the Chicago winter for a few weeks and also wanted to learn some ideas from us about the seasonal operations.

As soon as we met, we became great friends. Julie was one of the most authentic people that I had ever met, and needless to say I loved her immensely. During the weeks she was visiting, we spent a lot of time together talking about things in life that really mattered to us: family, friends, faith, religion, love and even death. We had many deep intense conversations. One reason I enjoyed them so much is because they were also full of intense laughter.

We both had a passion for finding out what "it's all about." She was full of life in every subject that we would talk about. She seemed to have such simple wisdom. When we discussed faith and the afterlife that is when we were set on fire!! We would spend hours talking about where would we go after we'd die. Would we meet the people we love after we pass over? What would it be like in the next life time? What are we learning in this lifetime? We would talk about the effect we have on every person we come in contact with, and how to make a difference. I loved being around her because she awakened that "something" inside of me, that was always there, just lying dormant.

I had just recently gotten married, and Julie was looking for a man to share a spectacular life together. We spent hours of laughing on how she was going to do just that. Our energy was contagious, wherever we were, people asked us: "How can we get whatever you guys have?" I felt as if she was the sister I never had. I didn't know it then but, we were meant to have this strong fast connection!

I enjoyed having her at work with me and hanging out with her on a daily basis. Soon she started feeling really tired paired with an annoying dry cough that was really bugging her. She wasn't feeling well so she decided to go back to Chicago to have her own doctor check her out. We all felt at the company that she was allergic to "the paper trees," and once she was back in Chicago she'd be fine. Boy, were we wrong! Terribly wrong!

Julie was diagnosed with Hodgkin's lymphoma. I wasn't even sure what that meant but, I knew I wouldn't be seeing her for a while because she had to start chemotherapy treatment very soon. She seemed to take the news like this was going to be an interesting journey.

As chemo progressed, we still had our wonderful conversations, but this time they were centered on treatments and her doctors. She was hoping that one of her doctors would fall in love with her inner beauty and just side step that bald head of hers. She was full of wisdom and insight and humor. Even on her bad days she would find strength in music, her writing and poetry which she loved. I could never get the messages of poetry, but she found a message in everything.

I saw her only one time after she left Florida. In between her hospital stays, we met for lunch in Chicago with another friend. We talked for hours and hours in a little café meant just for us. When we arrived, it was busy but the first time we looked at our watch, hours had passed and no one was there but the three of us. The wait staff was even vacuuming the floor, and we hadn't even noticed.

We were very excited because Julie was scheduled to have a bone marrow transplant. This would guarantee a full recovery, we were sure of it. Our afternoon together was full of hope with tears of laughter. When we said good bye, the three of us felt so alive, confident that everything was as it should be! But I was soon to understand why we had such a fast connection.

During this same time, my husband's job had transferred us to a different city in Florida, so I had to leave my awesome job, friends, my home and that beautiful beach!! But, soon after we were settled in our new place, I became pregnant with our first baby! We were so excited! A baby we had always wanted! But, I was feeling so sick ... with morning sickness.

My husband traveled a lot with his new job which left me alone most of the time. My morning sickness became afternoon sickness that ran into nighttime sickness. I was miserable! I would eat a little, throw up, and sleep. This was my pregnant life. If it wasn't for my dog, my best pal, and having to walk him, I don't know how I would have gotten up each morning! Thanks Murphy! I was so happy to be having a baby! I just wish I didn't have to feel this bad!

It was time to have my ultrasound to see the first pictures of our baby. Yeah! I could hardly sleep the night before. Everyone had told me that this is so awesome to experience then afterwards you'll be able to keep the picture. After the procedure, the technician said she would have the doctor call me and that I would not be getting a picture that day. Both my husband and I thought that was kind of weird. But as we left, we rationalized that since we were in such a small town, this must be the way they did things "around here."

Later that night the doctor called and told us there was something terribly wrong with our baby, and they needed to do more tests. Those tests confirmed what they saw on the first ultrasound: our baby had anencephaly and would not survive full term. Our baby would definitely not survive birth. We were devastated!

Is this why I had been so sick? I had a million questions. Julie, who was suffering her own illness with such grace, gave me comfort in the knowing that life works itself out. Everything will be as it should be ... Right?

I knew for myself that I could not carry our baby to full term. It felt in my heart the right thing for me was to let my baby go. With my husband's support we sought out the advice from my prior doctor. He felt it was the right decision, and said he would help us. I remember the day we had to arrive at the clinic, thinking to myself, this is the end of my pregnancy? I had always imagined that at the end of my pregnancy, there would have a beautiful baby in my arms that my husband had welcomed into the world with love and happiness. This could not be happening to me … but it was.

The staff greeted me with such love, tenderness, and without judgment. I felt in my heart that this was right for me but it somehow mattered to me that I not be judged. I was afraid that I was being punished somehow, and that as a result, I would not be able to have another child.

When the doctor and the nurses came into the room, the doctor came up to me, gave me a hug and told me that everything would be okay. They made sure I was comfortable. One of the nurses held my hand and wanted me to talk about how I loved my dog and how he loved me. With the tears running down my face, I talked about Murphy. When it was over, I sobbed, and they comforted me with compassion.

My husband and I had a quiet ride home. That night we lay in bed, held each other, and cried.

One night while I was asleep I had a visit from my grandmother who had died when I was 16 years old, but I knew it was more than just a dream. I was still grieving when she came to visit me on the foot of my bed. The words we exchanged were not spoken, but they were felt. She was there to comfort me, to let me know that everything was all right, and I should let go. As I awakened, her scent was all over me: on my hands, on my jammies, in my hair. The smell of cinnamon and sugar was around me. I know it sounds weird but, I felt the warmth of her healing love.

Friends came down to Florida to visit me and help me grieve. I felt very supported and loved. But deep inside of me I felt empty… Soon after, my friend Julie died. The bone marrow transplant had failed. Her funeral was a beautiful celebration of her life. It was her wedding into the kingdom of heaven. The music, flowers and the church were all arranged by her. She gave away her special things to each one of her friends with a special message on what we had meant to be a part of her life. Beautiful poetry was read while her

favorite music played.

As I sat in the pew listening, I finally understood the message in her favorite poem. I knew that this would make her laugh! I was grateful for our time together. I never thought our time would run out. As I sent her a message to seek out the soul of my baby and together watch over me, I knew after all of the conversations we had about death that she would and that she'd be beginning something new and wonderful.

After her funeral, I spent some time visiting my family. I would visit my dad who was now living in a VA hospital. He had had a lifetime battle with diabetes which had taken a toll on his health. He needed nursing care, and that is what our family could afford.

Our visit together was such a nice visit. We laughed at funny stories he told about what was going around him. He spoke such comforting words to me about losing my baby. I honestly had not expected him to say anything. It was a sweet time. When I hugged him good bye, I didn't realize that this would be the last time that I would see or hug him again. He died two months later of complications of his illness.

His memorial service was full of such fun and laughter. Many spoke of a man I didn't know, one who was joyful, loved to laugh, and lived for having fun with friends. His band buddies shared stories of what a jokester he was. A "happy-go-lucky guy," they said... I wish so much that I would have known that guy! For so many years I was mad at him for everything that he wasn't. Now I was hearing everything that he was to so many people.

After my father's funeral I went home, and we were transferred back to Ft. Myers. My main source of comfort was from Murphy. "My sweet boy" as we called him, Murphy was my buddy, my confidant, the one that kept by my side, gave me comfort. He was the first dog I ever had given to me from a friend of mine whose husband worked in the train yards of Chicago. A trucker was going to let this litter run wild in the train yards so my roommate took one, my friend took one and I took Murphy.

He was a black lab with the biggest head I've ever seen, way too big for his puppy body. I named him after a famous Chicago DJ, "Murphy in The Morning," because he was always barking to wake me up in the morning, and I thought the DJ had a big mouth too! Anyway, Murphy had an awesome personality. He would do the Scooby Doo talk. Since he loved to swim in the water, Florida was his heaven! I could not keep him out of our condo's swimming pool or the canal at the end of our street – which was scary because there was a gator living in that canal! When my husband would take him fishing in our canoe, he would sit up like he was a Native American and had been canoeing his whole life! Murphy was a great companion and friend.

Murphy started to suffer from epileptic seizures, and soon they became one continual seizure. The vet let us know that there was nothing he could do. So, within a month we let Murphy go.
In one year of my life I lost my baby, my friend, my father, my home, my job, and my beloved dog. Many days I was afraid what would happen next. Would I lose my husband? He's the only thing I have left!

Through these hard times I chose to try a focus on the goodness of each loss. I was meant to grow and become stronger, maybe to be more grateful to appreciate life.

I was happy to have known Julie and all the time that we shared. Those long incredible talks about life and death I felt a comfort and a knowing that death is not scary, it's a journey to the other side. Just because I can't see her doesn't mean she isn't with me. Julie taught me how life works itself out, and everything is as it is meant to be.

I am grateful for my husband who is always by my side to support and love me. My friends were supportive and loving, helping me while I was grieving my baby. I was excited to learn that my father had been a happy man in many periods of in his life.

I cherished where I lived by the beautiful Gulf of Mexico and the home in which I lived. I was feeling stronger and grateful! I felt powerful and soon I could laugh at how hard it had been. I made it through! I had grown in every aspect of my life!

Laughter Light

I have always loved to have laughter in my life and find the funny-ness of my life. This is not to say that I am always happy, smiling and laughing, but when I am at my best and living my life authentically, I am found in laughter.

My very first teacher, of course, was my Aunt. But when a friend gave me a copy of a book by Louise Hay called *You Can Heal Your Life*, this is when I started down a path of self-discovery and understanding. After reading Louise's book, I was hungry for more authors and books which would help me find the answers. I was a seeker to find wisdom about myself. I have read countless books of this type, and attended seminars, workshops, etc.

I found Michael Beckwith, Sonia Choquette, and David Hawkins to name a few. I loved the messages from Abraham/Hicks, Mike & Andy Dooley and, of course, Dr. Wayne Dyer.

Finally I had found the inspirational teachers I had been looking for!! I now realize that my whole life has been full of awesome teachers. I never left the classroom. My careers of different jobs, the different people that I met, people that still do come in and out of my life have taught me something about myself – all of it with equal importance. Sometimes I was not enjoying the lesson, wishing I could "drop" this particular class but, it is all unlocking my own wisdom to help me live my life in authenticity. It happens every day in every way, and for this, I am so grateful!

Being optimistic and finding that life was meant to be happy works for me. Optimism is a happiness magnet and with it, my life flows better. If I am positive, good things and good people will be attracted to me. I know this to be true for me.

When situations arise, I try not to get into the drama. I try to see everything with gratitude. What have I learned from this? Be grateful for the lesson and then find some humor in it! At times this can be really hard to see through the thick clouds. But being aware that whatever I need to see is for me, not against me, helps me find the humor.

Look at a picture of yourself when you are really laughing. You are beaming! Your eyes have the brightest sparkle! You are shining your light! ~ Your Laughter Light!! Notice this in everyone's face when they are laughing. It's the light of their soul and yours too! I just love that! Let our own light shine! It can start with a smile.

Choice

I love the messages from all of these inspirational teachers. I found that basically the messages are the same: You have a choice on how to live your life. You have the power to move forward no matter what setback or obstacles block your pathway. You have the power to attract the life that you want to live. You have the power on a day-to-day basis to be happy. You have the power in each moment how to react to others. You have the power to change your thoughts. You have all this power because you have the CHOICE. So, be authentic and make choices that support how healthy and happy you can be. Your life was meant to be happy! What are you waiting for? Laugh!

Cindy Ray

Dedicated to Donna "Mac" McDonald,
her heart was way too big for this world to handle.
Richard Cloud, my soul mate, who taught me more
about love than I ever knew. And my daughters,
Rebecca Chauff and Reagan Chauff, who give me
reason to laugh and to love every day.

Chapter 5
The Beautiful Truth

Chapter 5

The Beautiful Truth

Journey Back to Love

My journey back to love began on the day I was evicted from my life. Well, maybe not exactly evicted, but that's what it felt like when out of the blue my husband of nine years asked me for a divorce.

This came as a complete shock to me. He and I were best friends, business partners, lovers; our relationship had everything a great relationship contains. Or so I thought. I thought our relationship was so strong, we could make it through anything, and that we were going to grow old together. We were so comfortable with each other, we could be together for hours without saying a word – we could just "be."

We did the yard work together, cooked together, did home repairs together, shopped together, and talked on the phone several times a day when we weren't together. Even after being with him for over 10 years, I was still very much attracted to him.

We enjoyed a lot of the same hobbies and interests, all of the things that make a good marriage. He was the one I turned to when I had a problem or needed advice about anything. Even our last vacation was one of the best we ever had where we went crystal digging in Hot Springs, Arkansas with his daughter and some of our close friends.

Our life seemed to be very stable and happy. Even people who knew us thought we had the perfect marriage, and so did I. Well, maybe not exactly perfect, but really close.

But now, I had been rejected by my husband, the person who vowed to love me forever. This could not be happening! What about all of the plans we made together? What about the house that we were going to renovate and retire in? What about our personal growth business in which we were partners and taught marriage and relationship classes together? How ironic was that?

For many months, I cried and begged him to try to work it out, all to no avail. When that failed, I gave up and made the divorce very easy for him. We used the same attorney and settled the property between ourselves, pretty much giving him everything we owned, including the house.

People told me I was crazy for not taking him to the cleaners. But I didn't want to be "that person" who fought over lamps and the silverware. In fact, I didn't want to fight with him at all because I still loved him very much and wanted a peaceful ending. We had seldom argued during our marriage, and I sure didn't want to start now.

I came to the realization that "stuff" meant little to me anyway once I lost what was more important. I could replace the "stuff" that I owned, but I couldn't replace my family. His daughter had lived with us, and I was her mother for over ten years. My two daughters, who were 18 and 19, moved out, too. I missed all the girls terribly, and it added to my pain.

It felt as if my husband had died, and I was grieving the death of our marriage. Even after the final divorce papers arrived by certified

mail, the reality of divorce didn't sink in. I was unable to open the envelope for over a year but kept it sealed and tucked away in my safe.

I had a contract to teach classes at the women's prison. After we separated, suddenly, without any warning, the group that was paying me to teach cancelled my contract, so now I was teaching for free. I had no income, no house, no health insurance, no money, no family. Every aspect of my life was affected and felt very out of control.

Over the years, I had helped many women find housing and jobs and a new life. But now I realized that I had become so dependent on my husband to help me solve problems that with him gone, I didn't know how to even begin to help myself. I always thought of my husband as my best friend, the one I could be with and talk about anything. Now, on top of having no income, no house, no health insurance, no money, no family and no husband, I didn't have my best friend to help me through this crisis in my life. Our friendship was one of the things I missed the most with him being gone.

There were some really dark days when it took everything I had just to get up and get dressed. I experienced such profound sadness that there were times when I didn't want to live another minute. Fortunately, I waited for that minute to pass. And then another. And then another. Pretty soon, the desire to die would subside. Somewhere inside me, I knew if I could just hang in there for a little while longer I would be okay.

So, why did my "perfect" marriage end so abruptly? I would like to say it was because of the typical things that couples divorce over, money or sex, but this was not the case. I had lied to my husband about paying a bill that I didn't actually pay. Of all the reasons he could have given me, this was the reason he said he wanted a divorce. His explanation was that he felt betrayed and could no longer trust me to be honest with him.

I was astonished! How could all the years we spent together, everything we had gone through together, all our "HISTORY"

together, mean absolutely nothing? We had attended many relationship workshops where we bonded and became very close. My gosh, we were helping lots of other couples make their marriage work with the tools we taught. Why weren't those same tools working for us?

How could my whole world be ending and just go up in smoke over one lie? I didn't understand why he couldn't just forgive me. It was especially difficult to explain our divorce to others because not only didn't I understand the reason myself, I felt foolish saying it was because I lied about paying a bill.

In my heart, I knew that it was not the lie that ended my marriage, and there was something else that he wasn't telling me. But why wouldn't he just tell me the real reason? My friends suggested he must be having an affair because there's no way he would leave me for telling a lie. I knew there was more to it but the truth wasn't revealed to me for a long time.

Even though I kept asking him, he insisted the only reason was my betrayal. I couldn't accept that because it was easier for me to put the blame outside of myself. I blamed him for not trying, for giving up on our family, for breaking his vow to love me no matter what, and for not forgiving me. But blaming him wasn't getting me what I wanted: I wanted to stop hurting; I wanted my broken heart to heal; I wanted to be happy again.

I considered that maybe it was me who didn't love him enough, and not the other way around. I considered that maybe it was me that had wanted a divorce. But even a year later, I couldn't accept that, because I still felt that he had walked away with hardly a glance back. However, deep down, I knew that the failure of our marriage had nothing to do with him, and everything to do with me. All of the answers were inside of me, I just needed to keep looking.

It would take over a year before I was willing to stop blaming my former husband and others, take responsibility for my part in what happened and begin my journey of self-discovery. At that point, my whole life changed, and the life of passion and love that I was meant to live began.

The Story of Mac and Me

My story is dedicated to my friend, Donna "Mac" McDonald. Mac and her partner and my former husband and I were all best friends.

Our collective dream came true when we began a personal growth business together. For over seven years, we facilitated weekend seminars to help people regain their personal power and heal their relationships. But this dream began to unravel when both couples separated, and the business was closed.

I lived with Mac for a little while after my divorce. Since we were both life coaches, we would have frequent talks trying to identify what went wrong, and what were the core issues that contributed to the failure of both our former relationships.

Mac was also one of the most thoughtful and giving people I had ever known and would find little ways of showing this. One time she had given me a ring with little hearts on it and told me that every time I looked at it on my hand, I would know someone loved me. When the time came that I moved out of her apartment, she packed me a goodie bag full of things she knew I liked to eat so I would have them for my new place.

During one of our talks, Mac asked if I thought she was pretty. She also confided her belief that she was meant to be alone, and that she would never find love again. Another time she mentioned her fear of dying alone. This was all so incredibly sad to me since even though Mac had a huge heart for others, she wasn't able to feel that love herself, and never felt good enough, pretty enough, skinny enough or worthy enough of finding love.

A few weeks after I moved out, Mac's worst fear came true: She died alone as a result of taking her own life.

I was devastated and felt that I had let her down by not recognizing that she was giving up hope, by not trying hard enough to help her see that her self-worth and lovability wasn't dependant on how pretty she was, how much money she made, or how much she did for other people. How could I not see the signs? I "knew" her despair because it mirrored my own. Why hadn't I tried harder?

After her death, I was determined to do whatever was necessary to find the answers so that no one else would ever feel that dying was better than living - so that I would feel that living was better than dying. This story is her story and it is my story, and if it is your story, I hope it helps.

Beliefs

My whole life had been turned upside down because of my belief system about men, about relationships and about myself. All of us make decisions about men, women, ourselves, and life when we are children. Those beliefs become a part of our makeup and who we are. We see everything in our existence through the lenses of our beliefs that we form before we are seven years old. My journey included discovering my own personal beliefs then making a different decision about these beliefs that would help me in all of my relationships.

I studied Adlerian psychology while in school to become a Life Coach. Adlerian psychology is a growth model which stresses a positive view of human nature. It teaches that we are in control of our own fate and not a victim to it.

I knew the mechanics of the belief system and how to help people see the patterns that disrupt relationships. I thought I had already handled the blocks that had caused my failed relationships before this marriage. I thought I had made it through the tough years with him and didn't see how my beliefs were affecting our marriage.

He had issues too, but I couldn't work on his belief system. The only path for me to find happiness was to work on myself but I didn't know where to begin. Fortunately for me, I have a friend who is also a life coach and she helped me with much of it.

The breakthroughs came to me in segments. One day while I was in the grocery store, something occurred to me as I placed a carton of

eggs into my shopping cart. I wondered if anyone would ever love me for life, stay with me for good, no matter what, even if I kept making mistakes. At that moment, it was like God spoke to me right there in the grocery store. He said, "No, because you don't expect anyone to."

Suddenly I was flooded with the memories of my mother leaving me when I was 16 years old, and I actually recognized how unloved I have felt for decades. I wasn't worried about how to survive. My mother had done a great job of teaching me how to take care of myself, and when she left, she knew she wouldn't have to worry about me. She had confidence in me that I never had in myself. But if my own mother couldn't love me enough to stick around, how could any other person possibly care enough to stay with me?

My life coach had been telling me all along that my issues with my husband originated with my mom. But I was so hurt and angry that I was unwilling to even look at that belief again. I was so tired of hearing my own story, and I didn't want to tell it one more time. I didn't get it until that day at the grocery store.

Now I was curious about how this had affected my entire life. I wanted to know how many of my decisions had been based on my feelings of inadequacy and feeling unloved. I knew that my mom loved me, the problem was that I couldn't feel it. I kept reflecting and started remembering more of the details.

We moved a lot when I was younger, and when she left, I wanted to remain where I was living at the time so I could graduate from the high school I was attending. I had a choice of whether to go with her or stay by myself. She didn't "abandon" me, I made the choice to stay. It just felt like being abandoned because that was my perception. She made many attempts to keep in touch with me by sending me cards and letters. I never wrote her one single time. I didn't make one phone call. "I" was the one who withdrew the love from her and for the first time, I saw that.

This breakthrough changed my life. I realized how I had misunderstood the whole situation and tried to blame her, when it was really my own choices that I was angry about. I realized that love only flows outward. The times that I felt unloved was when I stopped being a loving person.

I could see how this belief directly affected my marriage. I was afraid to tell him the truth about the bill I didn't pay because I was afraid he would leave me like my mom did. So I withdrew my love from him. That was the betrayal he felt: the withdrawal, not the lie! He didn't feel loved. Why would he want to stay married to a woman who didn't love him? It was beginning to make sense to me, but this was only a piece of the puzzle. I had to keep looking.

The classes I taught at the women's prison four days a week was to be the source of more insight for me. One class in particular stood out to me. Almost every woman in the class had been abandoned by one or both of their parents. Some had been put up for adoption, and others were raised by relatives but this experience had affected all of them in a negative way. None of them knew how to get past it, and many of them chose to cover their feelings with drugs, alcohol, or other addictions, which led them to their arrest.

I was in a room full of hurting, helpless women who didn't know the first thing about how to change their thoughts about being abandoned. One woman's mom had left her on the library steps when she was an infant, so she had no way of finding out who her mom is, much less why she abandoned her. What if their parents had died? How could they find peace without ever knowing the truth of the situation? Most of them thought that knowing why they were abandoned would give them closure. But some knew why, and it still didn't bring closure.

I had to find a solution that didn't involve the parents. The answer had to lie inside of them. Inside of us. I could see that there was a connection and reason that so many of the women in prison had similar backgrounds.

I had a lot of discovery left to make about my belief system.

Why is it that there are about 7 billion people on the planet, and the opinions that affect us the most are from our parents? Why does it matter what our biological parents think of us? It matters because

we decide that it does. We assign our parents the roles of the givers of our love. We expect them to provide us with everything that we need, including providing for our physical needs and praising us. Even if our parents are no longer in our lives, everything we do is a result of how they loved us, or didn't love us, when we were children.

Most of us have never known that there is another way to get everything that we need, which is to go straight to the source instead of creating a middleman!

Do You Know What's in Your Love Recipe?

Every relationship is always affected by what is in our own unique "love recipe." By love recipe I mean the beliefs we learned about love when we were children. Our very first love was with our parents. From that original experience of "love," we formed healthy or unhealthy beliefs about what love is and how to get it. We make decisions in our present life based on how we felt and things that we observed when we were children. We will continue to recreate those patterns and cycles the rest of our lives, unless we consciously make changes to our love recipe.

For example, if you were loved and nurtured as a child, you will have a much different love recipe than someone who was abused or neglected. But, once we discover what ingredients comprise our own unique love recipe, we can add or take out the ingredients that don't work for us!

The attachment to the opinions of our parents is one reason that it is hard to be self-reliant when it comes to getting love. Because we are nurtured for eighteen years, we think that the rest of the world is going to give us what our parents did for so many years, good or bad. If only our parents had taught us that they were the middlemen, simply giving us the love that was already inside of us, then we wouldn't put the expectations on others to do for us what we can do for ourselves!

If you made changes to your love recipe, what would your life be like now? How would it be when you go to work and you don't have misguided expectations of your boss (parents), or co-workers (siblings), or employees (children)? If you could just be with them and work with them, and they added a savory flavor to your recipe instead of making it bitter.

How would it be in your intimate relationships if you had the freedom to really be yourself, without an agenda, without the neediness of a little child? If you had the freedom to express yourself without fear of disapproval or backlash? If you had the freedom to give love unconditionally because your love bucket is overflowing? All love comes from the self; it can only be given. If you think about it, don't you feel warm and "glowy" when you are expressing love to someone else? How do you feel love anyway?

My instructor and mentor, Mr. Bill Reidler, would always say that you can make a relationship work with anyone no matter who they are. At the time I didn't really understand, but I get it now. A relationship works if you choose to continue to send love out. If I cut off the flow, I stop feeling loved. When my mom left, I stopped the flow. That's why I couldn't feel loved by her. I stopped loving - not her. When I cut off the flow with my husband, I stopped - not him. One of the reasons I was able to give my ex-husband all of our material possessions was that I knew he was not the source of my income, just as he was not the source of my love and happiness. I am my source, and I create my life.

Who are you waiting on to make you feel loved or happy? How long are you going to keep waiting before you decide to be self-reliant and make those things happen for yourself? When you stop expecting others to do for you what you can do for yourself, you've taken the first step toward creating self-reliance.

When I depend on what other people think of me, I am allowing them to influence what I think of myself. Having the thought that my mom didn't love me was causing me to feel unloved but that was never the truth. It was just how I saw myself. When I started being self-reliant, I could see how everyone loves me.

When I was looking for happiness and validation from outside of myself, I was disappointed. For example, all of the sacrifices I made for my children when they were young were wasted on them. They didn't appreciate all of the things I gave up my career for: the school functions that I attended, field trips I chaperoned, functions I baked for, times I volunteered at the school, etc.

I thought giving up my life for my children was being a good parent, but it left me feeling unappreciated and resentful because I did it all for the wrong reasons. I know they were grateful that I was there for them, but not like I expected them to feel and certainly not like I expected to feel.

My feelings were a huge indicator that I was looking for validation outside of myself. I used self-sacrifice as manipulation to get the attention and love of others. I thought that all of the work I did should at least earn me that much. My attempts to earn the "right" to be loved were not successful, no matter how hard I tried. I helped homeless women find housing. I helped people move when they got evicted. I was helping my children. I was helping my husband. I was spending all of my time helping others. At the end of the day, what was left for me? I just felt tired of helping and giving to everyone else.

A prime example of how I tried to manipulate and pressure my ex to make me happy was when I asked him to buy me a hammock for our back yard. The year we moved into our new house, I asked him for the hammock as a Mother's Day gift. When I didn't receive it, I was very disappointed and resentful.

One day it occurred to me that I could have easily gotten the hammock for myself. I didn't really need HIM to get it for me. I realized how much resentment I was holding onto because of that one item, something that I could easily get for myself. I wonder if he felt the pressure of trying to please me and then not succeeding? I know that on some level, he must have felt the disappointment and resentment. I can only speculate on how much that $49 item actually cost me in the long run.

After he moved out, I bought a hammock for myself and now spend many hours a week in "my" hammock. I feel truly self-indulgent when I am gently swinging in the breeze. This became my favorite place to meditate or take an afternoon nap. I had the power all along to make MYSELF happy, but I was looking for the love and happiness to be "given" to me.

Now, I'm not saying that giving to others is a bad thing. What was causing me to feel used and exhausted was not the "act" of giving. My "motive" for giving is what caused me to feel used and exhausted. It is not what you do, but why you do it.

My 'why' was what was kicking me in the butt. So, I started delegating more responsibility to members of my team. I began to share the responsibilities instead of trying to do it all myself. And, most importantly, I changed my purpose for why I was doing the work I was doing.

I wish I had known then what I know now. I wouldn't have put my desires on hold for my children. You see, when you don't live your dreams, you cannot be an inspiration to others. When I started going for what I wanted, I became a positive role model. Of course, at first, my children, my family and my friends were disappointed that I wasn't there for their every need like I had always been. But they all moved past it and began doing what we all should do! They started living their own lives.

Your Love Threshold

I used to tell my children, "Nobody loves you like you do." I said it many times but never felt the true meaning of it until years later. I believe that we all have a "love threshold" that tells us when we have all of the love that we will ever expect to get, then we shut off the flow of any more love to us.

The truth is that no one will ever love you a single ounce more than you love yourself. If you find yourself repeatedly ruining what seem like good relationships, you probably have a very low love

threshold. You will only allow yourself a certain amount of love and happiness before you reject it.

Looking back, I can now see that is another way that I disrupted my marriage. On reflection, I can now see many ways in which he showed me that he loved me, and I could see all the ways that I pressured him to show me he loved me instead of seeing all the ways that he already did. I can only imagine the hurt I must have caused him every time I rejected him.

My love threshold became lower after my divorce, and I was even less willing to accept love from others. I shut myself off from friends, family, and anyone that wanted to be with me. I truly felt that I didn't deserve love. Only when I began to love myself did my love threshold raise higher.

If you find yourself in relationships with people who treat you very poorly, you probably have a low love threshold. Overcoming the opinions of our parents takes a lot of work. As does becoming self-reliant and making decisions about life from a mature mind instead of the mind of our inner children. The result is worth the work; YOU are worth the work. When you really get it that you are creating your life, the life you create will be more amazing than you ever dreamed possible!

Unfortunately, most of us get into this mind trap that it is other people making us feel loved, when in reality, what we are feeling is the good vibe that we are sending out. We make ourselves feel love, not someone else. The other person is only the mirror, reflecting back what we are sending out.

I am working hard to overcome the rejection of divorce. What I am realizing is that he couldn't reject me. I rejected him, and more importantly, I am the one who rejected myself! We think that love is outside of us but just as no one can make you angry, no one can make you feel loved. The love is inside of us, we just have to tap into it and let it flow from us, outward. That is real love. My ego was looking for love outside of me so I could find passion; what I discovered was that my heart had all of the love it needs, now and forever.

Moving On

A few months after the divorce was final, I began a relationship with someone that had attended the same high school that I did. We began communicating on Facebook, and discovered that we felt the same way on a lot of things. I was living in Louisiana, visited him a few times, then I moved to Florida to be with him and eventually we moved in together.

This was before I had had a lot of the breakthroughs and insights, so I still had some lessons to learn and things to work out. This relationship was very intense and unexpected. I had given up on love and didn't think I would find it, especially so soon.

Our relationship was difficult for me to explain to people. He and I didn't have all of the things in common that I had with my ex, and the relationship felt very different. Because my love threshold was so low at the time, I could not receive all of the passion and love that he expressed to me. Instead, I was overwhelmed by the love he showered on me, because I really couldn't believe that someone could love me so intensely. We fought a lot, and it seemed that we were doomed for failure.

I later realized that I was afraid to become comfortable with him. I had been very comfortable with my ex-husband and was blindsided when I didn't see the divorce coming. I was afraid that if I became too comfortable in this new relationship, I would get blindsided again.

One particular day that we spent together stands out in my memory. We had the most magnificent day and connected on a heart level that was beyond anything I had ever experienced. It was so spiritual and magical that I believed he was the one I wanted to spend the rest of my life with.

Later that night we had a silly fight, and out of the blue, he told me to leave. We had spent such a beautiful day together and connected on such a deeply intense level that I guess it was too much love for both of us to comprehend.

Beyond Beautiful

Once again, I was in shock, and I packed up my car and drove back to Louisiana. This is when I moved in with my friend, Mac. I lived with her for a few months before finding another place to live. After she died, I made a stronger effort to finish this book and share my story.

However, there were days when I wondered how I would be able to do it because I felt as unworthy as she had. I didn't know if there was anything that would make me special enough to prevent me from following in her footsteps. I felt severe pangs of guilt because of the belief that I didn't do enough to help her, which only added to my feelings of being undeserving of love. My love threshold was lowered even more.

Even though I was back living in Louisiana and he was in Florida, we stayed in touch and decided to work things out. I loved him deeply and wanted it to work. However, being apart proved too difficult for both of us. One day during an argument, he broke up with me. I couldn't believe it, dumped again! What was wrong with me?

By this point, I was having the breakthroughs and thought I had "fixed" myself. So why was this happening again? I am a very loving and giving person. Why couldn't I hold on to any relationship? Was I picking the wrong men?

I felt like I was on a roller coaster that was headed down way too fast. My head was spinning. Maybe I was being too pushy? Okay, I can change. I can do better. I know better. Hadn't I learned anything? I felt completely out of control and very anxious.

I assumed the worst. I tried calling him to talk things out, but he wouldn't answer any of my calls and messages. I felt more out of control. More fear. Why won't he just talk to me? Now I'm feeling like the desperate, crazy, psycho ex-girlfriend. I'll leave one more message. Maybe he will answer this time. Nope.

Maybe he's seeing someone else. My old abandonment issues were right in my face. Again. I could clearly see the patterns I was recreating, but I felt helpless to change them. I couldn't bear the

thought of going through this again, especially with him. I felt a bond with him that I have not felt with any other person.

I knew I was creating the experience because I could remember having thoughts earlier in the day that precipitated the flow of events. I had the fear-based thought that what I had written about him could possibly cause us to break up. Wow, I really am creating all of this!

I assume. I doubt. I fear. I get angry. I stop the flow of love. Do I really know what is going on with him? No. From the "victim" state of mind that I was in, I could not create the outcome that I desired. Something had to change.

So, I became very still. I calmed myself down with a short meditation and focused on my breathing. I stopped over-thinking the situation and stopped envisioning a future that I didn't want. This is not about choosing the wrong man. This has nothing to do with him. Once again, this was about me letting fear stop the flow of love to him. This is about my threshold of allowing love. This is about my belief system.

Why am I choosing this again? Is this what I really want? Am I pushing him away because I don't want him? No, that's not it. I do want him. Now what? Surrender. I let go of any agenda I had for him and our relationship. If my thoughts went to feeling sad or worried, I would ask myself, "Are you being a victim right now, or are you creating what you want right now?"

There were times in our relationship when I broke up with him, too. It wasn't always him breaking up with me. When I was getting dumped was when I felt the most out of control. It was when I was dumping him that I felt the most IN control, with no mystery to solve about what I had done wrong. So it was the times when I was getting dumped that were ultimately more beneficial for my healing.

I had to constantly remind myself that I was the one in charge of my happiness, not him or anyone else. I let go of trying to be in control. I thought about all of the things that I loved about him. I just thought about how much I loved him.

Send Out Love to Feel Love

When I imagined myself allowing his love to flow into me, I relaxed then felt a tremendous relief and a little happiness. I went about my day, not giving all of the drama another thought. If it didn't work out, so be it. I knew I would be okay. I know I am loved. I know that I am enough. I felt very peaceful and happy.

Not long after, he emailed me, then he called me. We came back together for a short while, but ultimately decided to go our separate ways.

I learned a lot about myself from this relationship. I learned that it doesn't matter whether I am with someone or not, it is self-love that is the most important love. So I will focus on and practice loving myself and loving those around me. For now, that is enough.

Upon reflection, I realized that part of my desire to work through a difficult relationship was not about love, it was my need to be IN a relationship at my age in life. But to do this is to settle out of fear, and I do not need to settle!

I AM in a relationship – a relationship with God and a relationship with myself. I am loved by God, and I love myself. I feel completely full of love.

Who I am as a person is not defined by a marriage partner, my body, my skin color, the shoes I wear, my makeup, my hair products or even the clothes I wear for that matter! Who I am is a collection of all the experiences I have had during my lifetime. Who I am is how I love others, care for others, and how I love myself.

Sometimes if we find ourselves floating in the wind, not knowing where we will land, just hang on and keep floating. We will end up exactly where we are supposed to be!

I realized that if I were ever going to understand all this love stuff, I had to do it for me. I couldn't help Mac, and I didn't reach all of the women in my classes. They didn't want my help, and I couldn't make their issues my own. The guilt feelings I experienced made me feel I was doing something about it when I really wasn't. Worry is not action. It just feels like it because it takes a lot of energy.

So I began to take real action, I started looking for the answers. Action dissolves fear. I felt my love threshold rising as I started focusing on what I wanted for me. I began to think about what I wanted, instead of what I didn't want. I find that when I am having moments of feeling completely out of control, if I meditate I feel much more calm and peaceful. Focus on the now, what is right in front of me. If I am in the now moment, there is no pain, there is no heartache.

The first thing to do is to stop the negative thoughts, just focusing on breathing and nothing else for a while. Then I was able to take the next step, to surrendering the ego and just "be." What if there is some bigger, better plan for me? Wouldn't I want that instead of this pain? Surrender to the higher plan.

When I am feeling anxiety about my future, I am actually setting up a scenario that I do not want. I have to surrender my control and see where I am led to go. When I surrender my pseudo control, it all works out for the best. Control isn't real anyway. I can't control anything anyway, that is just my ego trying to take over. When I surrender and let my Higher Self run the show, I am living from my authentic self. I am calm and serene. I think positive thoughts and create a future that I want. Then I express gratitude for all of the things that I already have. Being thankful increases what I am thankful for.

I wrote some guided meditations to help me speed up the process of changing how I saw things. They included meditations for self-love, allowing abundance, releasing unconscious un-forgiveness, weight loss, and self-confidence. I knew I had issues that I was not consciously aware of, and things that I had forgotten which were still buried in my subconscious. The meditations are designed to work with that part of the brain, where old stuff is stored.

Love Arsenal

We are all on a journey for love. Everything we do is about getting love because nothing feels better than to love. It doesn't matter who you love, when you flow love outward, it all feels good. So how about sending some love to yourself? Self love is enough.

How you received love as a child is how you will expect it as an adult. Did your parents show you love by spending time with you, or buying you gifts? Maybe they hugged and kissed you and told you they loved you, or perhaps they baked cookies for you after school? However it was for you as a child is the same way you like to receive love in your intimate relationships. It is important that you let your partner know how they can let you know that they care.

When we get caught up in our ego, we demand that others love us back or love us in certain ways. The amount of emotional pain that I am in is equal to the amount of pressure that I put on others to make me happy. When I ask you to love me, that is my ego talking. We already have all of the love we will ever need, and when we are fully feeling our heart space, we know that we are love.

So, when you find yourself in need of healing, have a love arsenal handy! What are some of the things you do to love yourself? Write them down and keep it so you will remember how to bring yourself back from the pain. With practice, no one will ever hurt your feelings again, unless you choose to allow it. Read something positive. If you don't have something positive to read, there are thousands of videos on YouTube to help you focus outward from your pain. Abraham-Hicks, for example, has a wonderful selection of videos and books that will help you see the big picture.

Sometimes when we realize that we are the creator of the disruptions just as we can love ourselves to raise the threshold for allowing love to a high level, there can be a tendency to beat ourselves up for making mistakes. In my own case, I would think that after all, I teach this stuff, I should know better! Why do I keep recreating the same scenarios? I'm never going to get this. My self-talk was very negative, and I needed to forgive myself.

We all have had a lifetime of creating negative thought patterns, so it will take some time to re-write the script that you have been reciting to yourself. No one talks to you more than you do. You wouldn't let your best friend talk to you the way you talk to yourself! We have over 60,000 thoughts per day. How many of those are negative? Monitor your self-talk and only say positive things about yourself and others. You know when you have made a mistake. Calling yourself names and punishing yourself does not undo or change the mistake. This only decreases your self-love. You have to practice loving yourself every single day. Pampering yourself is only the tip of the iceberg. I am talking about showering yourself with the love and forgiveness that you have waited for your entire life. Every single day set an intention to feel loved, and take the time to love and forgive yourself. You will be able to be more loving to others when you feel loved as well.

Forgiving yourself for your mistakes is very important for your peace of mind. When you feel un-forgiveness for yourself, that is the time to fully give unconditional love to yourself and others. One clue that you have unresolved un-forgiveness for yourself is that you may punish yourself in ways that are completely below the conscious awareness. Are you accident-prone? I have seen many people who subconsciously create getting themselves sick or hurt as a way of punishing themselves. (Although some people will intentionally hurt themselves, this is not the same behavior I'm referring to.) Looking for the beliefs or thought patterns behind this behavior is necessary to change the outcome. When we have unconditional love, we want the best for ourselves.

When I think back on my marriage, and how I gained about 75 pounds during the 10 years we were together, it occurs to me that if I was so happy, why did I need a substitute for love? The answer is, because my beliefs were preventing me from feeling loved by my husband so I substituted food to fill my need for love. Our belief systems are many-layered, and I was just beginning to see the connection between my marriage and my weight.

In one of the weekend seminars that I attended, one of the exercises was ranking people by how much money they had. I was somewhere in the middle, not too bad. Then the instructor told us to

sit in the chairs and rank ourselves by our weight. I knew I was not the heaviest, so I truthfully told my weight first. After everyone else gave their weight, I was at the back of the line, the heaviest person in the room.

I was so angry! I knew there were at least two people who weighed more than I did. It took me a while to get back into learning mode for the class after this because I just couldn't release my anger that the other people lied about their weight. Later I asked the instructor what happened. She told me that the reason this situation happened was because I felt like the fattest person there. My thoughts became what happened in that microcosm. What a revelation to me that just my thoughts about how I look compared to other people could produce such an outcome. I was not overweight as a child. I became overweight as an adult because that's how I felt.

All of Our Pain is Self-Inflicted

We all feel like frauds who don't want the world to see who we really are, so we all wear masks. Our fear is that if someone does get close enough to take our mask off, they will see us exactly how we see ourselves. But the gift is that they are our mirror, reflecting back how we already see ourselves. We must forgive ourselves if we are to change how they see us.

If someone is causing you pain, look inward to see what you need to forgive yourself for. Look inward to see why they see what they see, then thank them for showing it to you. They are your greatest soul-teacher. You owe them gratitude for helping you to forgive yourself. This won't be easy at first. It is so easy to point out that someone else is being mean or hurtful. This is giving them power to create your life. Get your power back by looking inward. Forgive them, then forgive yourself. Forgiveness is the key to inner peace and self-love.

My journey to overcome food addiction went along with my journey back to love. They both had the same basis in my belief system. When we feel love for ourselves, we want to do what is healthy for our bodies. But the hunger for food that I felt was a hunger for love. We think we are filling ourselves up with something that will satisfy us so we eat comfort food, or food we were denied as children (my personal favorite). But using food in this way will only satisfy us for a very short period of time. Then we have to go seeking more food, only to repeat the cycle of feeling unfulfilled, and beating ourselves up for eating yet again.

All of these moments add up to depression, weight gain, and negative thoughts about our appearance but does nothing to change ourselves or how we see food. We hate how we look, but are powerless to change it. How can I love myself when I look this way? How can I love myself when others look at me, judging me and what I eat?

The first thing you must do is to forgive. Do you see a pattern developing here? Forgive the person who withheld the food when you were a child, or forced you to eat foods you didn't like. How many hours did you sit at the table, forced to eat everything on your plate? They probably thought they were helping you, and making you healthier. But we only saw the situation through our child lenses. We don't know the real truth of the matter.

It was only recently that I realized when my mom was being critical of my weight, or not letting me have a lot of sweets, she cared about my health and was concerned for me. That thought took a while to sink in because of all the years I had been angry with her for the comments about what I ate and how I looked. I could only feel the hurt, I couldn't see the love and concern.

Once you quit blaming the other person, you will be able to choose what you eat, instead of being driven by your feelings of eating the opposite of what you were forced to eat as a child. If only my mom had withheld carrots and broccoli from me! Isn't revenge funny? We are killing ourselves to get back at the people who only loved us and wanted us to be healthy in the first place. Twisted.

Now, I could clearly see the belief pattern was similar to my views about love. It was all how I saw myself. The forgiveness is for you, for your peace of mind. Do it for yourself. Let go of your resentment about food. Stop seeing yourself as a victim of food. You are fully in control of the choices for what you eat. If you don't think you are,

  Beyond Beautiful

then you are a victim.

Like my beliefs about love, my belief about food has many layers, too. My unconscious revenge to my mom was to embarrass her by becoming overweight. I am the only one of her children who has a weight problem. Children see any attention as love, even negative attention. I got attention from being the only one with a weight problem. When I am feeling my personal power and self-love, I do not need that attention. Therefore I do not need the weight to attract it. I see myself so completely differently now, and it makes it easier to keep losing the weight. It also helps to keep me motivated to exercise on a regular basis.

A very valuable tool that I used in my weight loss journey was visualization. In the guided meditation I wrote, I go into detail about how to use the mind to help how I see myself and therefore create how I look. I made a vision board of what I wanted to look like when I reached my goal weight. I cut out pictures of women that I desired to look like. I also had pictures of me when I was thin that I added. Then I would take a few minutes each day to visualize what I wanted to look like.

If you were thin in the past, remember what it felt like. Think about how much more energy you had and how you felt so much more vibrant. Do this visualization every day if it applies to you. Take a few minutes and dwell on the good feelings that you had by being in good physical condition.

What type of language do you use when referring to yourself? Do you often call yourself fat, even in jest? Your subconscious brain does not know the difference between a joke, a lie, or the truth. That is what makes the meditations and visualizations so powerful. You can change how you see yourself and how you actually look by using these techniques. Take care of how you speak of yourself. Say only positive things about your weight and how you look. Remember, people will see you how you see yourself. Show them the real you, the person that is pure love and magnificence.

The Beautiful Truth

My intention for sharing my story with you is so that you will feel more encouraged about your life, yourself, and how you see the people in all of your relationships. I started out writing a very different story about love. Could I have learned all of this without having to put myself through a devastating divorce? Probably. But I didn't know how to do it any other way, so I did it how I did it. I know I have much more to learn about love and forgiveness. Hopefully I will not disrupt my whole life again to learn new things! I hope that you are gentle with yourself during your self-discovery. Learn some, forgive some, love some. You are already enough. You are pure, unconditional love. That is the beautiful truth.

About the Authors

Nancy Newman

is a licensed *Heal Your Life*® Coach and Workshop Leader/Teacher
with a private practice, Mindful Wellness, in Spokane, Washington.
She is also an author and speaker empowering people throughout
the world to live their authentic lives by sharing her personal stories,
facilitating workshops, and teaching the tools for healing, loving
yourself and discovering the peace within.

Nancy is also a certified Reiki Master, Reflexologist, and registered
Master Toe Reader. She enjoys traveling to Portland, Oregon to
spend time with her son, daughter-in-law and new grandbaby,
London Ava.

www.yourmindfulwellness.com
nancy@yourmindfulwellness.com

Lisa A. Hardwick

is an expert in holistic inner child healing, a licensed *Heal Your Life*®
teacher, author, speaker, workshop leader and a board member for
her local chapter Children's Advocacy Center in East Central Illinois.

She resides in Charleston, Illinois, where she enjoys spending time
with her three adult sons, her family and friends. She also enjoys
traveling throughout the world, sharing her testimony and assisting
others on their path to an authentic and beautiful life.

www.lisahardwick.com
lisa@lisahardwick.com

Elaine Lemon

is the founder of Empower Wholeness LLC, an Advanced Certified Practitioner of Neuro Energetic Kinesiology and the Energy Kinesiology Association. She is a spiritual, health and wellness coach, and also specializes in distance healing. Elaine is an Earth Transitionspractitioner. She is a certified and licensed *Heal Your Life®* workshop leader and teacher. Elaine is also a facilitator and instructor of Karlfeldt Healing Retreats.

Elaine currently lives in Boise, Idaho where she enjoys nature and living life with her five children and friends. Motivated by her own journey of health; she has embraced many modalities to empower others' healing and awakening to the beauty within. Elaine also loves traveling around the world, learning the healing arts and experiencing new cultures.

www.elainelemon.com
elaine@elainelemon.com

Robyn Podboy

is a National Workshop Facilitator, *Heal Your Life®* licensed workshop leader, a freelance writer and poet. Robyn lives her life through the eyes of optimism and humor, helping others shine their own light of authenticity. She grew up in a northern suburb of Chicago, IL and now resides in Ohio with her husband and two boys. She enjoys traveling, spending time in the sun and laughing with her family and friends.

www.shineyourlightnow.com
robynpodboy@aol.com

Cindy Ray

is a certified Life Coach and Parenting Educator through the International Network for Children and Families. She is a certified facilitator for the Fragile Families Program and has taught personal growth, marriage, relationship and parenting classes in the local prison for over seven years.

She resides in Baton Rouge, Louisiana near her two adult children, Rebecca and Reagan. She is surrounded by lifelong friends and family in her Southern community. She has a passion for gardening, traveling and helping others discover their true magnificence and their heart's desires.

www.Lifecoach123.com
lifecoach123@live.com

Beyond Beautiful

RESOURCES

The following list of resources are for the national headquarters; search in your yellow pages under "Community Services" for your local resource agencies and support groups.

AIDS

CDC National AIDS Hotline
(800) 342-2437

ALCOHOL ABUSE

Al-Anon Family Group Headquarters
1600 Corporate Landing Parkway
Virginia Beach, VA 23454-5617
(888) 4AL-ANON
www.al-anon.alateen.org

Alcoholics Anonymous (AA)
General Service Office
475 Riverside Dr., 11th Floor
New York, NY 10115
(212) 870-3400
www.alcoholics-anonymous.org

Children of Alcoholics Foundation
164 W. 74th Street
New York, NY 10023
(800) 359-COAF
www.coaf.org

Mothers Against Drunk Driving
MADD
P.O. Box 541688
Dallas, TX 75354
(800) GET-MADD
www.madd.org

National Association of Children of Alcoholics (NACoA)
11426 Rockville Pike, #100
Rockville, MD 20852
(888) 554-2627
www.nacoa.net
Women for Sobriety
P.O. Box 618
Quartertown, PA 18951
(215) 536-8026
www.womenforsobriety.org

CHILDREN'S RESOURCES

Child Molestation
Childhelp USA/Child Abuse Hotline
15757 N. 78th St.
Scottsdale, AZ 85260
(800) 422-4453
www.childhelpusa.org

Prevent Child Abuse America
200 South Michigan Avenue, 17th Floor
Chicago, IL 60604
(312) 663-3520
www.preventchildabuse.org

Crisis Intervention
Girls and Boys Town National Hotline
(800) 448-3000
www.boystown.org

Children's Advocacy Center of East Central Illinois
(If your heart feels directed to make a donation to this center,
please include Lisa Hardwick's name in the memo – she would be most grateful)
616 6th Street
Charleston, IL 61920
(217) 345-8250
http://caceci.org

Children of the Night
14530 Sylvan St.
Van Nuys, CA 91411
(800) 551-1300
www.childrenofthenight.org

Covenant House Hotline
(800) 999-9999
www.covenanthouse.org

National Children's Advocacy Center
210 Pratt Avenue
Huntsville, AL 35801
(256) 533-KIDS (5437)
www.nationalcac.org

Beyond Beautiful

CO-DEPENDENCY

Co-Dependents Anonymous
P.O. Box 33577
Phoenix, AZ 85067
(602) 277-7991
www.codependents.org

SUICIDE, DEATH, GRIEF

AARP Grief and Loss Programs
(800) 424-3410
www.aarp.org/griefandloss

Grief Recovery Institute
P.O. Box 6061-382
Sherman Oaks, CA 91413
(818) 907-9600
www.grief-recovery.com

Suicide Awareness Voices of Education
(SAVE)
Minneapolis, MN 55424
(952) 946-7998

Suicide National Hotline
(800) 784-2433

DOMESTIC VIOLENCE

National Coalition Against Domestic
Violence
P.O. Box 18749
Denver, CO 80218
(303) 831-9251
www.ncadv.org

National Domestic Violence Hotline
P.O. Box 161810
Austin, TX 78716
(800) 799-SAFE
www.ndvh.org

DRUG ABUSE

Cocaine Anonymous National Referral
Line
(800) 347-8998

National Helpline of Phoenix House
(800) COCAINE
www.drughelp.org

National Institute of Drug Abuse
(NIDA)
6001 Executive Blvd., Room 5213,
Bethesda, MD 20892-9561, Parklawn
Building
Info: (301) 443-6245
Help: (800) 662-4357
www.nida.nih.gov

EATING DISORDER

Overeaters Anonymous
National Office
P.O. Box 44020
Rio Rancho, NM 87174-4020
(505) 891-2664
www.overeatersanonymous.org

GAMBLING

Gamblers Anonymous
International Service Office
P.O. Box 17173
Los Angeles, CA 90017
(213) 386-8789
www.gamblersanonymous.org

HEALTH ISSUES

American Chronic Pain Association
P.O. Box 850
Rocklin, CA 95677
(916) 632-0922
www.theacpa.org

American Holistic Health Association
P.O. Box 17400
Anaheim, CA 92817
(714) 779-6152
www.ahha.org

The Chopra Center at
La Costa Resort and Spa
Deepak Chopra, M.D.
2013 Costa Del Mar
Carlsbad, CA 92009
(760) 494-1600
www.chopra.com

The Mind-Body Medical Institute
110 Francis St., Ste. 1A
Boston, MA 02215
(617) 632-9530 Ext. 1
www.mbmi.org

National Health Information Center
P.O. Box 1133
Washington, DC 20013-1133
(800) 336-4797
www.health.gov/NHIC

Preventive Medicine Research
Institute
Dean Ornish, M.D.
900 Brideway, Ste 2
Sausalito, CA 94965
(415) 332-2525
www.pmri.org

MENTAL HEALTH

American Psychiatric Association of America
1400 K St. NW
Washington, DC 20005
(888) 357-7924
www.psych.org

Anxiety Disorders Association of America
11900 Parklawn Dr., Ste. 100
Rockville, MD 20852
(310) 231-9350
www.adaa.org

The Help Center of the American Psychological Association
(800) 964-2000
www.helping.apa.org

National Center for Post Traumatic Stress Disorder
(802) 296-5132
www.ncptsd.org
National Alliance for the Mentally Ill
2107 Wilson Blvd., Ste. 300
Arlington, VA 22201
(800) 950-6264
www.nami.org

National Depressive and Manic-Depressive Association
730 N. Franklin St., Ste. 501
Chicago, IL 60610
(800) 826-3632
www.ndmda.org

National Institute of Mental Health
6001 Executive Blvd.
Room 81884, MSC 9663
Bethesda, MD 20892
(301) 443-4513
www.nimh.nih.gov

SEX ISSUES

Rape, Abuse and Incest
National Network
(800) 656-4673
www.rainn.org

National Council on Sexual Addiction
and Compulsivity
P.O. Box 725544
Atlanta, GA 31139
(770) 541-9912
www.ncsac.org

SMOKING

Nicotine Anonymous World Services
419 Main St., PMB #370
Huntington Beach, CA 92648
(415) 750-0328
www.nicotine-anonymous.org

STRESS ISSUES

The Biofeedback & Psychophysiology
Clinic
The Menninger Clinic
P.O. Box 829
Topeka, KS 66601-0829
(800) 351-9058
www.menninger.edu

New York Open Center
83 Spring St.
New York, NY 10012
(212) 219-2527
www.opencenter.org

The Stress Reduction Clinic Center for
Mindfulness
University of Massachusetts
Medical Center
55 Lake Ave., North
Worcester, MA 01655
(508) 856-2656

TEEN

Al-Anon/Alateen
1600 Corporate Landing Parkway
Virginia Beach, VA 23454-5617
(888) 425-2666
www.al-anon.alateen.org

Planned Parenthood
810 Seventh Ave.
New York, NY 10019
(800) 230-PLAN
www.plannedparenthood.org

Hotlines for Teenagers
Girls and Boys Town National Hotline
(800) 448-3000

Childhelp National Child Abuse Hotline
(800) 422-4453

Just for Kids Hotline
(888) 594-KIDS

National Child Abuse Hotline
(800) 792-5200

National Runaway Hotline
(800) 621-4000

National Youth Crisis Hotline
(800)-HIT-HOME

Suicide Prevention Hotline
(800) 827-7571

Bibliography

Agape Media International (AMI) and Sounds True

Beckwith , Michael Bernard.
    "The Life Visioning Process"

Benson, Herbert. (1975).
    The Relaxation Response.
    New York, NY. Harper Torch

Braden, Gregg. (2008.)
    Language of the Divine Matrix and Divine Matrix: Bridging Time, Space
    Materials and Belief

Canfield, Jack (2005).
    The Success Principles: How to Get from Where You Are to Where You
    Want to Be.
    New York, NY: Collins

Chopra, Deepak, M.D. (1990.)
    Magical Mind, Magical Body: Mastering the Mind/Body Connection for
    Perfect Health and Total Well-Being. Niles, IL.
    Nightingale-Conant Publishing.

Choquette, Sonia.
    The Answer Is Simple... Love yourself, Live your Spirit
    Hay House

Cohen, Alan.
    "Create A Masterpiece; When mistakes turn into miracles."
    healyourlife.com. N.p., 31 Dec. 2010. Web. 13 Mar. 2011.

Crane, Patricia J. (2002.)
    Ordering From the Cosmic Kitchen:
    The Essential Guide to Powerful, Nourishing Affirmations. Bonsall, CA.
    The Crane's Nest.

Duerk, Judy.
    Circle Of Stones: Woman's Journey To Herself
    LuraMedia

Eldredge, Emily.
    "Running Through the Fire." Awakening Path. N.p., 13 Sept. 2008.
    Web. 13 Mar. 2011. www.awakeningpath.com/articles/goodie_emily_
    el_080912_running_through_the_.htm

BIBLIOGRAPHY *(cont.)*

Gilbert, Daniel. (2005).
    Stumbling on Happiness.
    New York, NY. Vintage

Gilligan, Stephen. (1997).
    The Courage to Love: Principles and
    Practices of Self-Relations Psychotherapy.
    New York, NY. W.W. Norton &Company

Goleman, Daniel. (1995).
    Emotional Intelligence: Why it can matter more than IQ.
    New York, NY: Bantam Dell

Hay, Louise L.
    (1982.) Heal Your Body. Carlsbad, CA. Hay House, Inc.
    (1984.) You Can Heal Your Life. Carlsbad, CA. Hay House, Inc.
    (2002.) You Can Heal Your Life Companion Book. Carlsbad, CA. Hay
        House, Inc.
    (1991.) The Power Is Within You. Carlsbad, CA. Hay House, Inc.

"Inspirational Quotations by Alan Cohen."
    alancohen.com. N.p., n.d. Web. 13 Mar. 2011.

Krebs, Charles, Ph.D.
    LEAP Workshops
    www.ileapusa.blogspot.com/2009/03/charles-krebs-phd.html,

Landrum, Gene. (2005).
    The Superman Syndrome: You Are What You Believe.
    Lincoln, NE. iUniverse

Lesser, Elizabeth.
    Broken Open.
    N.p.: Random House, 2005. Print

Lipton, Bruce H., Ph.D. (2005.)
    The Biology of Belief: Unleashing the Power of Consciousness,
    Matter & Miracles. Carlsbad, CA.
    Hay House, Inc.

BIBLIOGRAPHY (cont.)

McErlane, Sharon.
    A Call to Power: The Grandmothers Speak. Bloomington, IN:
    AuthorHouse, 2004. Print.

Millman, Dan.
    The Life You Were Born To Live. Tiburon, CA:
    HJ Kramer Inc, 1993. Print.

Morrissey, Mary. N.p.: n.p., 2009
    Life Solutions That Work, LLC. Print.

Neill, Michael. (2006).
    You Can Have What You Want:
    Proven Strategies for Inner and Outer Success.
    Hayhouse

Ruiz , Don Miguel.
    The Four Agreements
    Amber-Allen Publishing

Time, Space, Miracles, and Belief. Carlsbad, CA.
    Hay House, Inc.

Tobar, Hugo, International College of Neuro Energetic Kinesiology
    Workshops & Certification, www.icnek.com

Tolle, Eckhart. (1999.)
    The Power of Now: A Guide to Spiritual Enlightenment.
    Novato, CA. New World Library.
    A New Earth: awakening to Your Life's Purpose.
    N.p.: Plume, 2008. Print.

Truman, Karol.
    Feelings Buried Alive Never Die. Las Vegas, NV:
    Olympus Distributing, 1991. Print.

Two Wolves Fighting, Native American Proverb

Wolinsky, Stephen. (1991).
    Trances People Live:
    Healing Approaches In Quantum Psychology.
    Falls Village, CT. The Bramble Company

Williamson, Marianne. (2009).
    The Age of Miracles: Embracing the New Midlife.
    Carlsbad, CA. Hay House

A SPECIAL THANK YOU AND ACKNOWLEDGMENTS:

Nancy Newman

Thanks to the many teachers and mentors along my path for their wisdom and guidance, especially Louise Hay, Dr. Patricia Crane, Rick Nichols and Michael Tamura for helping me transcend my past. Thanks to Lisa Hardwick for her friendship and this awesome opportunity. And, thanks to my "twin" and best friend, Mavis Hogan, for showing me that it was okay to let people into my life again.

Lisa Hardwick

To all of my devoted readers, my family and friends – I am filled with such gratitude for your support and love.

Elaine Lemon

To my beautiful children – Bryce Lemon, Alyssa Lemon, Derek Lemon, Connor Lemon, McKell Lemon – I love you forever. I AM in deep gratitude and honor for those that have supportively walked my path of healing, learning and awakening. Likewise, I feel blessed and honored for those that I have been given the privilege and opportunity to assist in their healing, discovery and growth. We are one!

Robyn Podboy

With much Love and Gratitude to my loving husband, Tony Podboy, for your friendship, steadfast encouragement, and gentle guidance. To my son, Alex Podboy, for your love, encouragement and authenticity. You bring me such joy. To my youngest son, Nate Podboy, for your love, laughter, and my reminder that life is always fun! You make me laugh like no other. To Fran Blaesing, for your unwavering love and support. To Ann Ring, for your commitment to spiritual truth, authenticity, wisdom, love and friendship. To Gail Eckerling, for your long-standing friendship, wit and humor. And to Lisa Hardwick, for your inspiration, encouragement, humor and friendship. With your vision and dedication, our book became possible.

Cindy Ray

Thank you to my friends and family and everyone who helped me through the tough year of my divorce. I am especially thankful for Mr. Bill Riedler, my mentor for many years. My sister, Sheri Madden, my mom, Jeanette Beason and my dad, Max Madden. My friends: Roni Casale, Kelly Kleinman, Tanya Bozeman, Michelle Southern, Marsanne Golsby, Delene Cole, Jana Laurant, Georgia Duhe, Kim Lambert, Margie Ohmer, Mary and Ricky Porter, Ellie David, Nekesha Anderson, Jana Miller, Michelle Flessas, Tammy Johnson, Pam Dunn, Tyler Riedler and to Scott Huber for having the vision to see something better for us both. Also to Lisa Hardwick for having faith in me.

LOOKING FOR
CONTRIBUTING AUTHORS!!

Most people have a story that needs to be shared – could *YOU* be one
of the contributing authors we are seeking to feature in one of our
upcoming books?

Whether you envision yourself participating in an inspiring book with
other authors, or whether you have a dream of writing your very own
book, we may be the answer *YOU* have been searching for!!

Are you interested in learning how sharing your message will assist with
building your business network, which in turn will result in being able to
assist even more people?

Our commitment is to make this planet we call "home" a better place.
One of the ways we fulfill our commitment is assisting others in sharing
their inspiring messages.

We are looking forward to working with you. To see if this might be the
opportunity for *YOU*, email Lisa Hardwick at lisa@lisahardwick.com .

CPSIA information can be obtained at www.ICGtesting.com
Printed in the USA
266037BV00004B/6/P

9 780981 879185